1095

THE HEALER'S
HAND BOOK

THE HEALER'S HAND BOOK

A step-by-step guide to developing your latent healing abilities

GEORGINA REGAN · DEBBIE SHAPIRO

Photographs by Dave Godwin

Element Books

© GEORGINA REGAN AND DEBBIE SHAPIRO 1988

This edition first published 1988 by
Element Books Limited,
Longmead,
Shaftesbury, Dorset

Printed and bound in Great Britain by
Billings, Hylton Road, Worcester

Designed by Jenny Liddle

Cover photo: Michel Tcherevkoff/Image Bank

British Library Cataloguing in Publication Data
Regan, Georgina
The healer's hand book : a step by step
guide to developing your latent healing
abilities.
1. Therapeutic systems
I. Title   II. Shapiro, Debbie
615.8   R733

ISBN 1-85230-022-1

CONTENTS

ACKNOWLEDGEMENTS

The authors would deeply like to thank Michael Mann and Simon Franklin for their vision and support; and Eddie Shapiro for his constant inspiration.

Also: Element Books for quotes from Reshad Feild's book, *Here to Heal*; Harper and Row for quotes from Ashley Montague's book, *Touching: The Significance of the Human Skin*; and Alexander Lowen for the quote from *Bioenergetics*.

INTRODUCTION

The paranormal is usually presented or regarded as somewhat weird, off-beam, eccentric, or as just a product of the imagination; it must have a scientific explanation somewhere, even if it is not immediately obvious. Yet most of us know of someone who is psychic, who will predict events or warn us of a forthcoming meeting; or even someone who is a medium and seems to go into a trance, maybe speaking in a different language, "receiving" messages from elsewhere. Or we may know of someone who seems to have magic healing hands capable of calming any kind of physical difficulty and who is soothing and comforting to be with. Many of us laughingly dismiss the paranormal, yet we know and love these people and invariably turn to them for help when we feel weak. Even if we cannot explain what it is that they do, we know that it feels good.

People with paranormal abilities are actually very numerous, but they tend to keep quiet about their talents for fear of unsympathetic exposure. The "witch who lives in the house at the end of the lane" is one such example. Regarded with fear and awe, she may simply be growing herbs to use as medicines, or may be able to read another's mind, startling him by knowing what he is thinking. Society's fear of anything that doesn't quite fit into a precise view of the world thus tends to label such people as freaks. Interestingly, many of us not only know such people, but have also personally experienced the paranormal, especially when we were younger.

The innocence and openness of a child's mind, given the space to grow and develop without restrictions, will often be in touch with "unseen" realms of existence. There can be an ability to tune into plants or animals and to understand their needs, such as knowing which plants need watering and which ones don't, or what to do if a pet has been hurt. Children may talk about past or future events that they can have no factual knowledge about, as if these events were totally real to them, like one such child who told his mother that his sister was waiting at their garden gate for them. At the time the boy was an only child, but within a month his mother was pregnant and later gave birth to a girl. Another example was that of a 9-year-old boy, who, when driving across a bridge in a part of the country he had never visited before, calmly told his grandmother how the last time he had been there they had had to cross on a ferry, as the bridge had not been built at that time. He knew exactly where he was and pointed out particular landmarks that had changed since his "previous visit".

Such qualities in children can be alarming for adults unless they too are receptive to the paranormal, or have experienced similar inexplicable events. Taking this innocent knowledge with us into adulthood is not easy. As we grow, so we become more self-centred, our field of vision narrows, and our rational mind dismisses such experiences as a "child's imagination", not a part of the real world. Our greater sophistication does not allow for the irrational.

Since the 1960s there has, however, been a growing awareness and interest in different levels of experience. Slowly we are beginning to accept that not everything has a scientific answer. There are now physicists who are brave enough to acknowledge what appears to be an element at work in the universe that even they cannot fathom, and there are a growing number of research studies showing that the human mind is capable of far more than was previously acknowledged. The transmission of energy, as in healing, is one area beginning to attract a great deal of interest, as it seems obvious that changes do take place during a treatment, but science and orthodox medicine have a hard time understanding how or why.

As an example of these studies, in 1979, Georgina Regan was invited to undergo stringent computer laboratory testing in controlled conditions, by parapsychologist, Dr Hirishi Motoyama, of the International Association for Religion and Parapsychology in Tokyo. The results of these tests proved the existence of the healing energies not only being transmitted through Georgina, but also being successfully received by the client.[1] Ms Regan has also undergone scientific testing by Professor John Hastad, at the Department of Physics, London University. Here it was discovered that she could produce electricity for a period of time which scientists had thought impossible for the human brain to do.[2]

Alongside the growing interest in healing is the growing number of those who are now practising healing or calling themselves healers, and this number is expanding very rapidly. Much as this is to be welcomed, it also gives rise to a gentle note of caution, for in truth the one who is the healer is not the one giving the treatment, but the one receiving it. The power to regenerate is a power within us, not something imposed upon us from an external source. In other words, the client is the only one who can really heal himself, someone else (a practitioner) simply acts as an agent so that healing may take place. So in effect there is no such person as a "healer", but rather an agent, or transformer, one who can transmit energy to another and thus create a more energised environment in which healing may occur.

As our conditioned world tends to revolve around labels, professions and categories, so we have come to call such an agent for healing a "healer", which can then be very misleading, no less so for the practitioner himself than for the client. How easy it is to become self-impressed with the idea of being a healer; before long we have become almost as an angel, bestowing miraculous blessings on all those we touch! And soon we are having to charge high prices for a treatment, or enormous fees for teaching a workshop, where we share such privileged information as how to place one's hands on a head to help relieve a headache! This may sound slightly facetious, but it is only a small exaggeration. It is very easy to get carried away with self-importance, and to forget that a practitioner is merely a channel for energy to pass through, and that every one of us is equally capable of being such a channel.

The ability to touch and transfer energy can actually be as normal to our being as reading or writing, the only difference is that we have never been taught how to do it. There are no esoteric or secret teachings; becoming a healing practitioner is not dependent on having special powers. Rather it is simply a matter of learning how to become quiet within and surrender the ego, how to be free of selfish desires, and how to love unconditionally. Each of us is capable of far greater states of consciousness and power than we may realise. All we need is the confidence to discover ourself, the desire to grow and a clear direction to follow. This book outlines the steps necessary so that our own energies may be freed, for the benefit of all.

·1·
THE POWER OF TOUCH

A young child, staying with her grandparents for the holidays, had an upset stomach. Her grandmother told her to lie down and put her hands on the area of discomfort, just to hold them there and relax. It worked. Within a short time the pain had gone and the child was up and ready for her next adventure. Her grandmother had been a nurse, but this was no medical cure, rather an instinctive knowledge of healing; at other times, she would put her own hands on the child to soothe an area of distress. Touching like this brings ease, comfort and the release of tension. In so doing it loosens the constricted nerves and muscles that are hampering the flow of energy, and frees that energy to bring about a state of harmony, or health. It also brings a sense of confidence and reassurance, often lacking when we are in a state of dis-ease. Through common gestures such as putting our arm around someone or holding hands, we are showing we care and the person being comforted is loved and wanted. As illnesses frequently have a psychosomatic cause, so this reassurance through touch is sometimes all that is needed to bring about a cure.

We display our instinct to touch in times of distress far more freely with children; with adults there can be a fear that it will be interpreted as a sexual invitation instead of a caring gesture. Between a mother and child we see constant displays of healing through touch, from the simple kissing of a sore knee to the holding, cuddling and stroking at times of emotional upset.

From numerous studies [3] it has become apparent that touching is in fact essential for life, and that we can actually suffer mental damage or even die if seriously deprived of tactile contact. The most obvious example of this is at birth. We are all familiar with how animals laboriously lick their young immediately upon delivery, after which the newborn will usually struggle to its feet and begin to suckle. Unlike humans, animals have relatively short birth canals and delivery is therefore fairly fast. The licking process that then follows does far more than just dry the skin; it also stimulates the circulation of the blood, the respiratory and digestive systems, the nerves, and the endocrine system, thus effectively bringing the animal "to life". Without this licking (as when the mother dies at birth), the offspring can also die unless another animal, or a human, activates the same processes. In humans, the approximate eight to fifteen hours of muscular contractions during labour performs the same purpose as licking, as it stimulates the life-sustaining functions of the foetus ready for separate life. Premature or caesarean babies who miss this process, have been noted to be more susceptible to infectious illnesses, to lethargy, and to be slower in learning.

The importance of touch for the development of basic human qualities was portrayed in the English BBC Horizon film "A Touch of Sensitivity", produced by Stephan Rose in 1979. Research in this film showed what happens when physical contact is absent in early life, but when all other maternal acts remain present. In various experiments, baby monkeys were separated from their mothers by a sheet of glass for different periods of time, although they could still see, hear, and smell each other. One group was permanently separated, another group were parted for up to fourteen days at a time intermittently throughout their childhood. The first group, who suffered severe tactile deprivation, were seen later in life to avoid one another, to be aggressive in communication, have difficulty in co-operating, and to tend towards isolation, as they experienced tremendous problems with forming meaningful relationships. They became withdrawn, alienated, and unsociable. The second group, having experienced some tactile contact in controlled time periods and then denied it again, later became clinging and child-like in their need for touch. As if they had never fully matured, they were demanding, lacking in confidence, and extremely dependent. In other experiments with monkeys, severe brain damage was found amongst those who were totally isolated as well as amongst those who were only partially separated (this group had physical contact for up to four hours each day). In these cases, as above, all other senses except touch were fulfilled.

Further research in the film showed infants in a special care unit in hospital. Out of necessity, the conditions surrounding these children had to remain sterile, thus enforcing a lack of tactile contact with the child. However, in this particular experiment, infants were placed on a lambswool blanket for twenty-four hours out of every forty-eight. Over a period of time it became clear that the babies given this extra tactile contact were gaining weight faster, and displaying greater contentment, than babies not lying on the lambswool. On the day that the infants were thus placed, they would gain approximately 15 grams more weight than usual. The lambswool provided a form of touch and of tactile stimulation otherwise lacking.

We can also see how a lack of touch can cause great suffering not just in the young, but in the elderly as well. As Ashley Montague, in his book, *Touching. The Human Significance of the Skin* notes:

One has only to observe the responses of older people to a caress, an embrace, a handpat or clasp, to appreciate how vitally necessary such experiences are for their well-being ... it may be conjectured that the course and outcome of many an illness in the aged has been greatly influenced by

3

the quality of tactile support the individual has received ... one may suspect that it was the individual's history of tactile experience prior to his or her illness, and particularly during it ... that made the difference between life and death ... A perfunctory peck on the cheek is no substitute for a warm embrace, nor is a conventional handshake capable of replacing a caressing hand, the only touch of love.[4]

Touch can therefore be seen to be essential for the development of emotional security, confidence, safety, acceptance, and freedom from distress – all qualities that are vital for balanced growth. The modern society that we live in does not encourage touch, at least not in the Western world as it does in the East. There we find it normal practice that a child stay in constant physical contact with its mother or another adult for the first few years of its life; we find it natural for families all to sleep close together; the massaging of babies is an integrated part of their daily routine. In the West we have created a structure that actually denies touch, from the removal of new-borns to a separate room, the intervention of bottle and pram (instead of breast and sling), to massage being a 'red light' activity. As we have become alienated from touch, so we have lost the basic instinct of how to heal. In the face of medical science we have belittled the importance of human contact; instead of simply holding and soothing the head of someone suffering from a headache, we rather offer an asprin.

Healing through touch, i.e. the specific use of touch in certain areas to determine specific effects, is an innate talent we all have and can develop further if we wish. However, we are never taught how to do this and, until recently, the ability was even suspiciously thought of as belonging to the occult world. Yet the practice of healing in this way was an intimate part of the life of mankind throughout history, and was woven into the fabric of religions, philosophies, and lifestyles. For the tribal cultures, the healers were the most respected of their venerated persons. Those known to have special visions, dreams, or mediumistic abilities, were specifically chosen to be trained as healers or spiritual guides, as seen in the witchdoctors, kahunas, shamans, and medicine-men. The Judaic-Christian tradition mentions numerous Biblical incidents where human suffering was eased by someone supplicating the divine on their behalf, by the laying on of hands.

For many centuries man believed that his life was influenced by a dimension of existence beyond his complete knowledge and understanding. This unknown realm gave him a sense of destiny and purpose. So it was until approximately the third century AD when the organised Church decided that the age of miracles had come to an end. The Church claimed that God had allowed Jesus to perform miracles and healings in order to establish the Church in the minds and hearts of men. As that was now accomplished they were no longer necessary. Healing, which had once been an effective and integrated reality of early Christian and pre-Christian life, was officially stopped, frowned upon, and very soon ceased to be. If a person became ill or suffered great hardship, it was considered that they were therefore living lives inconsistent with the wishes of God, and were being punished for their sins. Unfortunately this consciousness still exists and underlies the morality and psychology of Western man. Touching has lost its importance and the isolated and lonely world we now know has taken root.

However there are strong indications that we are coming back to a deeper understanding of man's powers. Our cultural conditioning, our religious teachings, and the concepts of what actually constitutes reality, are under question. The image we have of ourselves as human beings is changing, as the vastness of man's mind becomes apparent. This change is reflected in a greater acceptance of the unexplainable, and includes the rebirth of healing.

We are now seeing a philosophy and understanding beginning to emerge that emphasises man as body, mind, and spirit, individual yet inseparable, and each intimately involved in the ability to maintain the health of the whole. Techniques such as affirmations (positive mental attitudes), meditation, visualisation, and deep relaxation are becoming well known methods of treatment, and the use of touch, as seen in numerous massage techniques, is now more widely accepted as therapeutic.

Massage has in fact developed at an extraordinary speed in just the last few years. There are now massage training schools in most major cities, with strict legal requirements, long apprenticeship hours and detailed anatomical and physiological study. In some areas there are more massage therapists than any other form of alternative practitioner. Many of these massage therapists are now also recognising that their work does far more than just relieve tension in stiff muscles. During a treatment – an hour of prolonged tactile contact – clients can experience emotional or mental release of past traumas; afterwards they may find illnesses that were not directly being treated, changing, if not actually dissipating. Massage is a technique designed to bring about physical ease in the muscles and tendons of the body. In so doing, it also frees the flow of energy throughout the body, calms the nervous system, stimulates the circulation, releases tension in the digestive system, and soothes areas where nerves and muscles are constricted. And this takes place even if the massage is very light and gentle. It is the touch, the relief such touch brings, and the increase in energy, that then enables inner healing (through a freeing of constrictions) to take place.

While having a massage treatment, it is not unusual to find the massage therapist quietly holding her hands on certain areas of our body; or for instance, we may find her holding one hand against the lower spine, and another on the foot, while we simultaneously feel a movement of energy through the leg between the two hands. This is healing through touch, and professionals working with the body, as massage therapists do, can find themselves instinctively touching in this way, even without prior training in such methods. It is entirely natural for our hands to respond to dis-ease through touching, and we often do it without even realising it. Massage is just one example of this. Others may be found in the numerous healing methods now becoming known, such as Therapeutic Touch (as taught to nurses in some of the hospitals in the USA, it works away from the body); Reiki (a Japanese name for the channelling of energy for healing); Shiatsu (the touching of specific areas to release energy along channels (meridians) in the body); and Polarity Therapy (a system for balancing the energy flow in the body through touch).

With the growing awareness of healing and complementary therapies, there is a parallel decline in confidence in the capability of orthodox medicine to deal effectively with ill health. Specialists in the medical profession are finding it harder to keep pace with the rise of chronic or "incurable" diseases, and the approach of treating just the sick part of the body without regard for the whole, can result in only a partial or temporary relief. But to move from the use of orthodox medicine to the use of natural healing methods demands a desire for a more holistic approach, and also the ability to take responsibility for ourselves. Most of us do not question authority. We believe that if food is being sold to us then it must be nourishing to eat, and when we get sick we presume that a doctor with his enormous array of medicines can make us well again. We do not take the responsibility to choose our nutrition, to employ preventive health measures, to discover the cause of our problems, or to heal ourselves, all of which we can do more easily and with more success than we might think.

Using touch to bring about healing is the simplest and

7

most natural form of therapy available and one which we can learn easily without extensive training as it is the direct expression of our humanness. Everything in the universe is made up of energy, so when we touch someone there is a natural transference of our energy to them. If the person is depleted of energy, or if it is hampered in some way (thus creating physical problems) then we can "give" energy and enable a rebalancing to occur. In this way we act as an agent so that healing can take place through the increase of vitality in the one receiving.

In essense we cannot heal anyone else, we can only heal ourselves, as our healing comes from within our own cellular structure – it is a regenerative quality as seen in the ability of the skin to heal over a cut. Someone else, i.e. a doctor or healing practitioner, can only act as an agent to create the right circumstances, the freedom within, for the body to heal itself. The pills a doctor administers will aid resistance so that the patient can fight an infection more easily. The healing practitioner, through touch, stimulates and adds to the flow of energy into the cells, and healing takes place by virtue of the additional strength and energy received. The body will then heal itself according to its own inner needs. What those needs are may not be known to the practitioner, and it is not important to him – he is not concerned with the external manifestations of dis-ease. A practitioner simply gives energy and the client uses that energy as required to bring about their own healing, as only within the client can there be a true knowledge of where and why there is an imbalance.

The energy that is transferred may simply be that of the practitioner's own energy, or it may be coming from him but not of him. This latter is known as channelled energy, and the difference between the two is an important one.

The giving of one's own energy to another is known as magnetic healing. This is because the practitioner lets his own energy be attracted to the client, as to a magnet, and it is what usually happens when there is the instinct to help someone, like when a mother holds her distressed child; it is a giving of personal vitality and energy reserves. It is a joy to give in this way and the one receiving feels better, soothed, and loved as a result. People who have abounding energy are naturally magnetic healers, and others will feel energised by them. However, when the practitioner's own reserve is depleted, then lassitude and weakness will follow, their health may be impaired and they may need "time out" in order to be replenished.

Healing effected through the channelling of energy does not result in such depletion or exhaustion. It is not a transference of our own energy, so there is no personal loss, and in fact such healing is usually revitalising for both the practitioner as well as the client. Channelled healing happens when the practitioner is allowing energy to flow through him – it is a transference of universal energy rather than relative energy, and there is no involvement on an individual level. The practitioner merely acts as an agent or transformer.

To heal in this way is far simpler than the terms imply, but it does ask of us such abilities as a letting go of ourselves and it further requires an awareness of other states of consciousness. On the other hand, magnetic healing does not demand anything of the practitioner other than good health. There is no need for self-surrender or deeper understanding, simply a desire to help. Many of us start with magnetic healing, will practise the simple giving of ourselves through touch, exploring the realms of energy and healing on a personal level. Invariably though, questions arise, feelings are experienced in respect of which we seek different answers, and we find we are being led on to an exploration of prayer or meditation, or to studying parapsychology or the esoteric sciences. All of this is essential for channelling energy, a practice which requires us first to look at ourselves. The next chapter will explore this more fully.

Channelled energy occurs when we are able to surrender, to let go of our own self-importance, our ego, and when we start to allow energy to flow through us without interference. It is in response to a deep love and compassion for our fellow man, and asks of us patience, honesty, and commitment. But it is something that we are all capable of doing. Channelling energy is not in the realm of the chosen few or of the esoteric eccentrics. It is simply a development, a conscious furtherance of our natural ability. We discover the importance of touch; we begin to recognise that by directing that touch we are having a healing effect; we see how we can give of our own energy for this purpose, but also begin to realise it need not be a giving of our own energy. And more importantly, that when it is not personal, then it is actually more effective, the results are deeper and more lasting, and the client's state of being is more fully energised.

Within us all, given the space and time to discover it, is a state of emptiness, wherein lies the divine. This emptiness is not a negative state, but rather a postive one, an emptiness that is quiet, peaceful, joyful, and revitalising. Divinity is the term we use to describe this state of peace, of oneness with life and from which all life manifests. It is not used in a religious sense, but rather to portray a state of consciousness beyond that which we are usually familiar with, and through which we find a level of fulfilment unobtainable in our normal world. Other terms that are often used to describe the divine are: the Higher Self, the Source, God, Cosmic Consciousness, or Grace. This state of inner peace can be directed through us. We channel energy but it is not our energy that we are channelling, rather it is the divine within us all. Our motivation is the compassion we feel, our strength is the joy that is inherent in the divine. When we learn how to heal therefore, we are not developing a "special gift", so much as discovering true peace within ourselves and learning how to share this with others. Patience and practice deepen our experience and our ability to attune to these energies.

Healing in this sense is far more than a purely physical

experience. It is a loving force that enables a releasing of the root cause of our illnesses. Whenever a practitioner "treats", he always has total confidence that a change is possible, as will happen when we receive love and allay our fears. It may not necessarily have a physical expression, rather the client may experience mental or emotional changes like the release of guilt or anger, but from such release healing can take place.

The realisation that healing through touch should be a normal expression of life is reinforced by the constant examples of healing that surround us in nature. Ironically, we have forgotten that we are also a part of nature and therefore equally capable of healing. When an animal is hurt it will try to find a quiet, dark place in which to rest, thereby freeing as much energy as possible for the healing process; it will fast, thus releasing the body from expending energy on digestion; and it or a fellow animal will lick its wounds for many hours, thus cleansing, soothing, and comforting. When we humans fall sick we do not know what to do. We lie in bed watching television (which can excite rather than calm); we eat ice cream (which offers little nourishment and wastes valuable energy on digestion); we off-load responsibility onto our doctor; or we stoically pretend we are fine and try to carry on as normal, ignoring the messages in our body. We have lost touch with our instinct. But just as we can laugh, cry, or breathe, so we can also heal. It is an inborn part of our being, a natural regenerative talent that all other forms of life take for granted.

By bringing together the laws of nature and the divine, we can easily go beyond our self-imposed limitations. We can move, be free of restrictions and repressions, can participate in life more fully. A seed needs the earth, rain, and sun in order to grow to its full potential. It uses these elements but the growth comes from within the seed. In the same way, we need food, warmth and a loving environment in order to grow. Touch is an essential ingredient of that loving environment. Just as the earth carresses the seed, so we need to be carressed and held. The power of touch can be seen in the effect it's absence has, for without it we become alienated and confused. With it we blossom and grow healthy.

·2·
GETTING STARTED

If we take time to look at the teachings of the world's great masters and sages, we find many common threads running between them. Invariably they speak of love, in its most unconditional and compassionate form, as essential for true peace and happiness. Through such love we find freedom from pain and suffering. Unconditional love is love without limitations, boundaries, or conditions. One loves another simply because one loves, not because the recipient does or is something special. The love is constant, regardless of what happens, because it is not based on specific needs or requirements being fulfilled. It is love for the sake of love. Compassion, or loving kindness, is the objective expression of unconditional love. There is no personal involvement, rather one is motivated to act through the depth of one's empathy and understanding.

Most of us live in a state of wanting, whether it be for material objects or the ability to control and manipulate events or people in our life. We want to be a healer, but that wanting may be coming from a place of personal desire. As we grow, we are conditioned by a world aimed at material and social achievement, suffering great pain if there is a loss of this, and exerting tremendous energy to maintain or gain further assets, power, or fame. It is not surprising that we take this conditioning with us even into the field of the healing arts, for the way of selflessness is a more demanding path to follow.

Desire is the motivating factor in life. Not having our wishes fulfilled creates frustration, anger, and restentment. If we were able to release our desires, then we could be free of this suffering. We do not need actively to stop our desires in order to release them, but rather to find fulfilment within, so that if external wishes are not satisfied then it does not matter. Our suffering is not, for instance, because of a lack of money, but because we desire more. If we can feel at peace within ourselves, then we can be content with what we have. We may still be in need of more, but the need does not upset our inner peace or create distress.

If we are to be truly effective in our work, then this is the direction we need to go in. To be able to channel energy we have to surrender ourselves and our desires, and this asks of us tremendous self-honesty. What is our motivation? Are we really able to love unconditionally? How important is it that we have more money? Do we ever really make time to be alone and look within?

LOOKING WITHIN

The sages not only spoke of unconditional love, but also of prayer or meditation. This is the act of quieting the mind, through which contact with our inner being and other levels of consciousness is reached. The scriptures offer us this practical path of contemplation as the way to selfless compassion. It is the tool we can use to understand ourselves further, to find the stillness within whereby our conditioning and suffering can be dissolved. It is the way through which we can discover our own divinity and the ability to share this with others.

So before we explore healing any further, it is important to establish the basis from which healing can function. As we saw in Chapter 1, if we wish simply to give of our own energy to another, then none of this is necessary. But if we wish to be able to help on a deeper, less personal level, then a clearer understanding of ourselves and the way to that understanding, is the basis of our work. We can help someone else only as far as we have helped ourselves. If we have not looked within and accepted with love what is there, then we cannot truly cause someone else to release their own unseen patterns of dis-ease. If we are not at peace, then we cannot expect to help another to discover their own peace. If we have not learned to listen to our inner voice, then we will not be able truly to hear someone else.

Healing therefore, starts at home. To begin any path of self-discovery, we first have to learn to relax, to truly relax whereby not only our body is at ease, but our mind also. Through such relaxation we create the inner space in which we can explore further. Most of us think of relaxing as stretching out in an armchair, putting our feet up and letting the world go by without our interference for at least a few minutes. Our body might thus be eased, but to allow our mind to relax also is not so simple. There is normally a constant chatter going on, filling every space available, and it is not really possible to try and stop this, for that trying is still the mind at play. Instead, we have to redirect our energy away from the mind and let go of the trying. This can be achieved through deep relaxation as described in Chapter 8.

Practising regularly creates a naturalness in our actions, just like learning how to drive a car or play the piano. It is the same for relaxation. As we relax, so we lose ourselves as we normally are and find ourselves in a new way. For this, it is very important to accept where we are starting from, rather than trying to do or be more than we are. In accepting, we learn to love ourselves for who we are now, not as we would like to be. By accepting and loving ourselves, without judgement, so we can also accept others and love them unconditionally, rather than trying to change them, or wish they were different.

As our relaxation deepens, so we may find unexpected experiences happening, such as visions of colour, light, or symbols; or the sound of beautiful music, or even the sound of an inner voice. Or we may find ourselves in a state of absolute quiet, so still it can feel as if we have almost stopped breathing. Whatever happens, we simply witness. As we are eager to gain material possessions, so we become eager to gain spiritual ones, to hold on to our experiences as signs of great power. But if we hold on to a signpost, we will not see the land the sign is pointing at. By letting go, the experiences deepen.

From relaxation we can move on to meditation. We do not have to relax before we meditate, but relaxation helps to put us in touch with the quiet space from which meditation grows. Meditation is not just sitting with our eyes closed and feeling peaceful – it goes beyond relaxation as it is a purposeful focusing within. Meditation actually develops in three stages, from concentration, to contemplation, and then to true meditation, a merging of self with the divine on an absolute level. We start with concentration, which has already begun to develop through the relaxation. There are many techniques for concentration and each of us will find that which suits us best. Whatever the technique, the idea is to give the mind an object on which it can focus, thus releasing the energy used in normal mental activity. The most widely practised methods are based on the breath. All life must breathe, and the rhythm of our breath reflects the rhythm of the universe. Through focusing, the mind can then become deeply concentrated, until even the object of the focus dissolves and we are left in a state of pure concentration. Through this we find ourselves at one with our divinity, and our egotistic self becoming less dominant.

As well as specific meditation techniques, there are also visualisation techniques and the use of sound (mantra). There are many forms of visualisation which can stimulate our creativity and can open the door to a wider perception. Suggested practices are explained in Chapter 8. Other tools we can use to quieten our mind and explore ourselves further are techniques such as yoga, t'ai chi ch'uan, or the martial arts. Yoga means union, to unite, to come together as one. It incorporates breathing techniques, relaxation, meditation, as well as asanas, or physical postures. These asanas are done with full awareness, slowly moving in different ways to stretch, strengthen and invigorate our whole being. In itself, yoga provides a complete system for the prevention of illness and the preservation of health, physically, mentally, emotionally, and spiritually. T'ai chi ch'uan is a Chinese moving meditation, a series of specific postures that are done very slowly, with absolute mindfulness, as a means for deep concentration. It also tones and stimulates the body so, like yoga, it incorporates both physical and psychological benefits.

LEARNING TO LISTEN

These practices are also a way to develop the ability to listen to our inner voice. Most of us experience this voice as intuition, a gut-feeling telling us something, often contradictory to what is expected. When we can purposefully tune into this voice we realise it is our higher self, an aspect of our being beyond our normal mind, that can point or encourage us to reach deeper understandings. As we are able to listen to our own voice, so we will be able to 'listen' to others. This means being able to tune into someone else on a different level. Not only do we usually find it hard to actually hear what someone else is saying, but it is even harder to hear their inner being speak. Yet within all of us is the desire to communicate on this deeper level and it can be an extraordinary relief when we realise that someone is really hearing, or "seeing" us.

We can further develop our sensitivity through simple techniques such as holding a stone, or touching a tree. All matter is made up of energy and even rock has a vibration we can feel. If we sit quietly with our eyes closed and hold a stone or pebble in our hands, we can feel its qualities and become attuned to this different perception. Shells and rocks are millions of years old and we can sense this, even visualise it, when we hold a stone in this way. Trees also vibrate with energy. Standing with our arms around a tree, or sitting with our back against the trunk, we can "feel" the energy of the tree flowing into us, we can become one with the tree. Or we can stand by the edge of the sea and, with our eyes closed, hear the sound of the surf, feel the water within our being. Try these exercises both before and after a deep relaxation or meditation and see the difference. They help us to become open to different vibrational rates, different manifestations of energy, and enable us to realise that life is not always what we perceive it to be. There are numerous manifestations of life we cannot always see, but we can feel them, see them with an inner eye, hear them with an inner ear. As we develop our listening and sensing abilities, so we can merge more easily with another human and will be able to "hear" their inner being speak.

ATTITUDE

In learning how to listen and how to channel, we also need to learn how to heal ourselves. If we are suffering from a definite physical problem then we may need to become a client for a while and receive healing therapy. But if we are relatively free of physical problems then it is our mental and emotional states that we should turn our attention to. When we are practising, we need to be free of stress, personal problems, and to be able to put ourselves "on hold" so that we do not influence the work being done. In between working with other people, we should therefore take time to work with ourselves, accepting our imperfections and turning our weaknesses into strengths. We are not perfect, if we were we would be enlightened! Instead we start from where we are and, from here, learn an attitude of honesty, understanding, humility, and of unconditional love, for ourselves as well as for others.

Being truly honest with ourselves and accepting what we find is not easy. What is our reaction if someone scratches our car? Or spreads gossip about us? If we get shouted at, do we get angry back? Do we get overburdened with worry? Do we get depressed easily? The response to any of these questions points at the desire for life to be different, that somehow it would be better if we had more materially, or lived with nicer people, or didn't have so much to do. This arises by looking for answers outside ourselves rather than inside. We may wish to change the world, but the truth is that if we change, then the world does too, for we then see it differently.

Our attitude to life determines how that life will manifest. Action follows thought. Have you ever noticed how people who live feeling persecuted and have a chip on their shoulder, always seem to have things go wrong? Whereas those who are optimistic and cheerful, never seem to get burdened with hardship? This is not so much because of fate but because of attitude. The same things can happen to us all, life is impermanent and full of obstacles, but our attitude is what makes an experience either positive or negative.

An example of this is that of two people, both of whom had cancer. A mutual friend was trying to explain how good nutrition had saved one of these two friends from dying. He related how the first one, on discovering she had cancer, became depressed. She did not change her life in any way and continued to eat the same diet as before. The second one decided that cancer was not going to beat him and immediately began exploring nutrition, changing his diet considerably. Within a period of time the first person was dying, while the second was recovering. The point their mutual friend had missed by focusing on their dietary intake was the difference in attitude. It was not just the food eaten that had made the difference (without doubt diet plays an essential role in creating and maintaining good health) but also the differing attitudes towards the illness. For the first one she felt she was going to die anyway, so there was little point in changing. For the second, he took responsibility for his own life and became positive in his approach to it.

Our understanding of life and fears related to that understanding will create either a sense of ease or dis-ease within us. As humans, we know that the future will at some point contain our death, and may also contain suffering and pain. There is naturally a fear of this, and therefore a fear of the future, of the unknown. To counteract this fear, we hold on to the past, for even if that past was traumatic, nonetheless it was relatively safe as we came through it alive.

The recognition that life is impermanent, that in fact all things are impermanent, is the only way really to overcome this fear, and is the most positive attitude we could have. It is a very joyful recognition, as it relieves the pressure. Does it really matter about material success, or is it not more important to open our heart to loving more deeply? Does it really matter what people say about us, or is it not more important to develop compassion? How long or short a life may be becomes irrelevant compared to the depth and meaning of that life. And that in turn may be determined by our ability to listen to our heart. The native Americans were known to have commented, when meeting white men for the first time, how strange it was as, "the white man thinks with his head instead of his heart". Thinking with, or listening to, our heart, opens the doors of wisdom. Our head may be far more logical and rational, but our heart is where our inner voice lies, and if we follow it instead of our head, it is invariably more rewarding. Our understanding of life expands and deepens in this way.

Through relaxation and meditation we can find this inner voice, emanating from a point of stillness, and it is from here we can express ourselves outwardly. Responding from this centre our attitude becomes balanced, free of ego, and able to be objective and non-judgemental. We do not have to be so subjectively affected, if something has upset us then we can replay the scene in our mind and see how different it might have been if our ego had not been involved. If we get depressed then we can recall other moments in our life which had felt equally depressing but from which we emerged joyful. There is just energy, it is our interpretation of it that makes it better or worse. If something goes wrong then we can look at the other side of it, and recognise all the benefits inherent in the situation, for nothing is entirely negative – the opposite is also always present. If we feel sad we can sit down and remember moments when we were very happy, times when we laughed a lot. As we recall that feeling we see how the sadness and happiness are simply dependent on our attitude at the time. We spend our life thinking we are being affected by external events, when in reality we are being affected by our own attitudes.

MOTIVATION

As we develop our understanding, we need not only to look deeper at our attitude, but also at our motivation for what we are doing. Obviously there is a desire to serve mankind in some way. There has to be this initial motivation in order to impel us to seek further. But do we also think of ourselves as the one doing the healing, as the healer? Do we respond to a request for help by saying: "I can heal you"? And even if we don't actually voice this, do we nonetheless feel we have a special power to heal?

The ego is extremely deceptive and self-honesty not always very comfortable. How easy it is to do something convinced we are doing it without thought of ourselves, only to find we are disappointed if it does not work as we had hoped. The disappointment then shows us how personally involved we really were. Ideally, it should not make any difference to us if a client gets better or not after a treatment, for it is not us who is doing the healing. Yet how often do we feel useless if a client does not make progress, and feel elated if they do? Either feeling is an indication of our attachment.

To be detached from what is happening is not a cold or uncaring state, rather one that reflects a deep level of compassion and humility, a surrender of self. The belief that we can heal is replaced with the deeper knowledge that we are only the agents for healing to occur. We cannot heal another, we can simply help create the right environment for healing to take place. The earth does not create the flowers that grow in it, it just provides the right environment. It does not react if a bud should not blossom, or if a tiny seed grows into a magnificent tree. It creates the environment for growth by just being there, not by doing something special; and it gets on with doing whatever it has to do regardless of what may manifest from its soil. Are we so easily at peace? Do we desire to bring change to another? Do we want to be thought of as having some special talent? And even if we accept that we are not the one doing the healing, do we not want to be credited with being the one channelling the energy, creating the perfect environment? How easily we delude ourselves!

When a client comes to us with a particular ailment, it is very natural to think of directing the treatment to the healing of that difficulty – we want him to be free of pain, so we do what we think is needed for a release to take place. However, when we do this we become personally involved by presuming that we know what the client needs. What we are not acknowledging is that it is only the person himself, deep inside, who can know what is needed, and this knowledge may not even be conscious. A physical trauma could be the result of an emotional or mental trauma that is locked away out of sight. If we try to dispel the physical pain, we are not creating the space for the deeper trauma to manifest and be released. If we focus on the symptoms then we are ignoring the causes. So always we treat the whole being, and allow the healing to occur without our interference. In this way we are tuning into the deeper patterns and not getting involved in the manifestations. "Our responsibility as healers is to be able to recognise the cause behind the cause that appears as the effect in this world, to recognise how the energy patterns work in the human body and in the land itself, and finally to recognise the hidden God that lies within each and all of us."[5]

Our motivation is also seen in our relationships. As we grow in experience and confidence as practitioners, so we may find we are getting a following, becoming a figurehead, someone others lean on for support and help. Clients can become dependent, calling often to talk or wanting to see us. Is this desirable? Having a following does not necessarily imply we are a clear channel, but it does imply personal magnetism and involvement. There is nothing wrong with working as a therapist or counsellor and it can be a natural extension of healing, as a treatment will often unlock hidden conflicts that need expression and an understanding listener. However, it is also important to encourage our clients to discover their own strength and to take responsibility for themselves. If we encourage dependency, we may be hindering them from finding an inner freedom, or their own potential. Instead of looking within themselves, they will be looking outside, at us, for answers. So if we begin to get involved with our clients, it is important to make a mental check, to look at our actions objectively, to ensure our motivation is not based on personal gratification.

DISCOVERING SELF

It must be obvious by now that there is a lot more involved in getting started as a practioner who can channel energy than just touching someone! It is in fact a path of our own self-discovery, as much as it is one that can stimulate self-discovery in others. As we set out on this journey, there are some basic items we need to take with us to ensure our survival and progress, such as meditation (so we may find the hidden signposts); a compassionate attitude (so we are able to accept whatever we may find); and perseverance (so we do not become waylaid by delightful distractions). We should also include an elementary understanding of anatomy and physiology, at least enough to know where all the major organs are and what they do (so we are familiar with our landscape). An understanding of other healing techniques and therapies also helps, as there may be times when we need different answers to the ones we have (such as times when it would appear that our client needs specific help like counselling or nutritional advice).

In starting out on our journey there also has to be a degree of fearlessness and self-confidence. In this case it is important that we have no fear of being in contact with serious illnesses, or of death, nor a difficulty in talking about such subjects. If the idea of this does not feel too comfortable, then it helps to know of therapists or counsellors we can recommend to our clients if need be. And we need to feel confident that we can undertake this journey, knowing there will be times of doubt and questioning ahead, as well as times of joy and clarity.

There will also be occasions when we are in need of energising, when the path becomes too steep and we need time to refresh ourselves. We can do this through relaxation, meditation, sitting quietly in the garden, or even by just going for a walk, maybe by the sea or through a wood. Oak and sycamore trees are particularly energising. Try sitting and leaning back against one such tree for a while and see what happens. We are a part of nature and can thus be energised through contact with our source. We also need to receive. As much as we can channel energy through us to another person, so we also need to receive energy for ourselves. Many people who give find it very hard to receive, yet in receiving we are creating the opportunity for others to give. Loving ourselves means being kind to and treating ourselves with the respect we treat others, not a neglecting of our own needs. Having a healing treatment or a massage is often essential so that our energy is able to flow freely and we can continue on our path.

Healing through touch is a natural expression of our human beingness. As we make the journey from what we are to what we may become, we discover extraordinary joy, a new awareness of life, a deeper understanding of all the unanswered questions, and a boundless, all-encompassing love. It is the joy of life itself.

·3·
EASE AND DIS-EASE

When we are ill physically, it invariably affects our approach to life, our mental and emotional stability, and we get feelings of frustration or hopelessness. Similarly, when we feel depressed, unhappy or angry, we usually suffer physically as well, getting a headache, nausea, or aching muscles; when we are happy and joyful, so our body feels more alive, vibrant and healthy. There is a direct interrelatedness of mind and body – one cannot be affected without the other. Action follows thought – as we think so we become. This point is an important one to recognise in order to understand further what is happening when we fall sick and recover.

Modern man is riddled with dis-ease; we have become so used to headaches, colds, constipation, or even cancer, that we have forgotten such sickness should actually be a rare event. Dis-ease has become so ingrained in our life that we mistakenly think of it as normal. We undergo numerous operations and consume vast quantities of medicines, to such a degree that our state of health has become the subject of hours of social conversation.We talk of physical problems as if they had little to do with us, were simply happening to our body, almost as if someone else had imposed the illness upon us. We "have" a physical difficulty like an unwanted possession. Yet it may also be a possession we are reluctant to let go of. Our illness becomes a companion and life without it, without having to go to the doctor, fill prescriptions, or have anything to complain about, is alarming. We have even reached the point, so totally out of touch with instinct and intuition as we are, where we believe that sickness is God's will, an accepted fact that is out of our control. Health is only for those lucky few who always seem to have good fortune anyway – they are not like the rest of us who have to suffer!

Although this is obviously a sorry state of affairs, the sadder fact is the apparent lack of intelligence we apply to recognising the relationship between health or sickness, attitude, and way of life. Because we do not acknowledge that the mind and body affect each other, we therefore cannot take this further step. Yet we are our body. We are not someone else's body, and we are not separate to our own body. Through our body we express ourself and relate to the world around us. Our body is our means for expression and it therefore expresses who we are. If our body falls sick then it is a part of us falling sick, it is not something separate to us falling sick. The dis-ease is an expression of an imbalance within our being.

However, as we cannot put our mind under a microscope, instead we put our cells under a microscope, and by focusing so closely upon the body we have lost touch with its integral relationship to the mind. For instance, we do not connect the need to communicate, to "get something off our chest" with the bad cough we have; instead we take a cough suppressant and suppress our inner conflict at the same time. We do not connect the tension or feeling of pressure in our shoulders with the long-held guilt we have; so instead, given time, the shoulders bow and we get back problems. And the guilt remains intact. Nor do we connect our inability to let go, or a lack of spontaneity, with constipation. Instead we take a laxative and carry on in our fixed patterns of behaviour. A deep fear or anxiety will soon begin to wear us down, deplete our enthusiasm and energy, until we lose our resistance and fall sick.

The relationship between mind and body is, in fact, so

totally integrated that there is virtually no state of dis-ease that cannot be traced back to a psychological or emotional attitude. Different areas of the body reflect different psychological states and there is a constant exchange of information throughout our whole being:

> Today there is strong agreement among the healing professions that illness stems from the mind, but it is also important to remember that the mind is made up of many levels. This is easier to understand if we return to the idea that we think and feel from different areas in the body, each area having its own special function. What we put out in thought will always come back and land in the same area where we tightened at that moment. The moment is ever-living, yet we trap it in our judgements, our fears and our illusions and thus we are not free. [6]

Dis-ease is on the increase because simultaneously our way of life is being threatened by ever greater pressures. Stress is the most basic factor stimulating illness. Stress is caused by frustration, anger, anxiety, hopelessness, fear, shock, disappointment, apprehension, grief, guilt, hatred, depression, uncertainty, pressure, loneliness, worry, obsession, despair, resentment, noise, and so on. Stress accumulates until it creates inner tension and constricts the muscles. Constricted muscles affect the flow of the blood and the functioning of the nerves. These in turn affect the glandular system. The maintenance of our entire physical system is dependent on the blood, nerves, and glands functioning properly. As they begin to deteriorate, so an enormous array of physical disorders develop.

If we can find the cause of the stress, develop relaxation, quieten the mind and discover a sense of inner peace, then the muscles can be eased. Then the constricted veins, arteries and nerves are free to perform properly again. Then the glands and organs are resupplied with essential nutrients. Then physical healing can begin.

As we cannot put frustration, anger, or guilt under a microscope, so orthodox medicine tries to help by bringing relief to disrupted organs and tissues, or by offering sedatives or anti-depressants. But this is not dealing with the cause of the problem. It is the covering of a crack in the wall in the hope that it will go away. To heal on a deeper level so that health becomes a natural state of being, means dealing with stress, the causes of that stress, and the effect it has had. Obviously a closer liaison between medical professionals and healing practitioners could only benefit us all greatly. Man is not just his physical body, nor is he just a mind. All aspects of his being are intimately concerned with the health of the whole, mentally, emotionally, physically, and spiritually.

It is interesting to note here another difference between natural healing and orthodox medicine. A doctor will have to listen to a description of his patient's ailment, and then through his knowledge of the human body, he can diagnose the problem. A healing practitioner however, can carry out a treatment without any knowledge of the complaint or area of difficulty, for the channelled energy entering the body will naturally go to the area where there is a lack of energy. If there was a diagnosis, the treatment would then concentrate on the problem, but the cause of that problem may not be touched, for it is deeper within. By not diagnosing the symptoms, we are allowing the energy to work without our interference – we are trusting in the process itself and recognising our role as simply an agent. Therefore the less our individual self is involved, the more effective and encompassing channelled healing can be.

Although orthodox medicine can undoubtedly help us and at times is obviously necessary, there cannot be this deeper healing without the release of the cause, the replacement of dis-ease with ease. The body is fully capable of recuperation, given the energy and impetus to do so. But the mental and emotional states we generate and maintain, hamper this process. Again we find ourselves coming to attitude and the effect of that attitude on our well-being. Surely we do not actually want to be sick? Yet no one inflicts illness upon us – it can only be manifested from within. Admittedly we may not do this on purpose, but it is us nonetheless.

Recognising the external stress in our life is relatively easy. Recognising stressful thought patterns is not so easy as most of us are not aware of our ingrained attitudes. If we were it is unlikely that we would perpetuate them, as none of us actually enjoy suffering. In fact, illness can be the most wonderful opportunity to see how irresponsible we have become towards ourselves and can give us a very real impetus to take responsibility to care and love ourselves again. "Healing means "to become whole", to be one with our Creator as we were at the beginning. It is what is meant by the words in the Bible, "to be healed of our sins", for a sin is really only a lack, a lack of knowledge, a state of sleep and forgetfulness. What a pity it would be if we were to pass through this life in such a state!" [7]

In the East, relaxation (through techniques such as yoga and t'ai chi ch'uan) and meditation, are considered normal, an integral part of daily life. In the West these activities are considered "fringe", but they should not be dismissed so lightly. Here we suffer greatly from stress, from cancer, heart disease, ulcers, depression and mental instability, to name but a few illnesses. Eastern traditions coming to the West in the 1960s and 70s may yet be seen to be our saving grace! Without relaxation the stress we experience soon causes severe damage.

If the mind can be aroused to a state of receptivity, of inquisitiveness, then progress can be made. The act of coming for a treatment is the first step. It is the indication that a desire for change is emerging. But the cause of the stress may be very deep and influencing us in many different ways. Therefore, concurrent with healing, there may also be a need for counselling, to enable these inner patterns to come to the surface and be recognised. This avoids a recurrence of the illness through unsolved problems. Mixing healing treatments with other forms of treatment (whether it be counselling, psychotherapy, acupuncture, osteopathy, or even orthodox medicine) is perfectly acceptable. A state of harmony is our goal. The means to reach it may vary. No one way is better or worse than another, each deals with a different aspect. Working together can create a whole.

EXPECTATIONS

The ability to recognise how we are creating our own illness shows itself in our level of expectation from a healing treatment. Many people come expecting a miracle, and if they are not healed in one session, will leave disappointed and scathing of the work. They are the ones who will spend an enormous amount of time and money searching for a miraculous cure, and spend virtually no time looking within themselves. So no matter what a practitioner does, the illness may persist. Any form of treatment received can only help us – it cannot do the healing itself. In receiving we also have to be willing to integrate the results, to allow a state of ease to penetrate, to be open to where we have been responsible for our own state of ill health, and to work at maintaining peace within.

One of the most interesting aspects of healing is that very often the client will not know (nor does he even need to know on a conscious level) what the inner cause of his problem was. It is resolved on a deeper, seemingly non-conscious level. Thus a client may come for a treatment because of a pain in his arm. Through the treatments, the pain recedes. As a result of this, he feels a tremendous release from tension, worry, and fear about the affliction. He becomes calm. The stress that originally formed the pain is released in the letting go of the stress caused by having the pain.

Generally, in the first treatment, there is a freeing of the energy within which brings a calmness to the nervous system, a balancing between the mental and emotional states, relaxation, increased vitality, and a cleansing of the blood. The muscles, tissues, fibre and bone are nourished and cleansed. In the following session the energy seems to penetrate more deeply, going more directly to the problem. Having first brought calmness and ease, so the body is then ready to begin the healing process.

That does not mean that "miracle" cures cannot, or do not happen. Here we mean a spontaneous healing in one session. They can happen, most often when the client is absolutely ready to move on, when he has already let go of inner stress and has only the lingering physical imbalance to remedy. It is beautiful to witness. But it is rare and sadly (due to media sensationalism) has created an aura around channelled healing so that others expect it to happen to them also. When it does not they are disillusioned.

Experience teaches us that although there can be such instantaneous cures, healing is usually an accumulative process. Dis-ease in the body may manifest as a simple headache that can be eased fairly quickly, but it more often manifests in the form of deeper conflicts. These will then need to be balanced before a physical change can take place.

Conversely, a complete cure may not always be achieved, especially if the illness has already reached an advanced stage and there is severe damage. However, as it is our attitude that underlies our state of health, so it is that healing can bring valuable help and energy to our psychological and emotional states. As our attitude changes there develops a general feeling of well-being. In cases of near death, the transition may even become one of ease instead of fear. An example of this was that of Susan, who had cancer in both her blood and bones, and who eventually did die. But the change in her as she received treatments was remarkable. Her personality went from being bitter and depressed to that of being loving and optimistic. There were some physical improvements, such as her hair began to grow again, and she lived for four months longer than expected, but the greatest progress was in her attitude. She died in a joyful positive state, feeling at one with God.

In less extreme cases, clients may not recognise that a treatment is being effective as it is working on levels more subtle than the physical. They do not notice that their breathing is calmer or their sleep patterns are improving, that their diet is changing or that they are no longer losing their temper as they did before. We expect immediate physical improvement and so do not pay attention to other changes as being a direct result of a treatment.

NO LIMITATIONS

Having looked at attitude and expectation, we are beginning to see the power of thought. Thought is the precursor of action. Ask and you shall receive. In asking for a treatment, so we are opening within and stating our intention to let go of the cause of our dis-ease. It is a surrender from which we are able to receive on an inner level. If we do not ask we remain closed and constrained by our own limitations. The act of asking enables the receiving to take place.

Wherever there is an imbalance of energy creating a state of disharmony, so healing can assist. It will equally help: marital or relationship problems (divorces have been avoided, families reunited); drug or alcohol dependency (clients may experience withdrawal symptoms similar to being in a clinic); mental difficulties such as schizophrenia, epilepsy, breakdown, emotional or psychological trauma (by balancing the nervous energies); or any one of the thousands of physical complaints from which mankind suffers.

We have come to think that there are certain states of being that are basically incurable, such as cancer, mental handicap, rheumatism, multiple sclerosis, and so on. This is primarily because orthodox medicine feels incapable of helping and so has labelled them such. But wherever there is life there can be change. Absolutely nothing is permanent. The cells in our body are constantly dying and being re-formed, so the opportunity for transformation is always present. There are no limitations, other then the ones we impose ourselves. If we deeply believe we can recover then we will. Our attitude determines the state of our cellular structure far more then we realise.

Illness is a state of constricted or traumatised energy; health is a state of free and peaceful energy. The difference between them is a clear one (and we can help convey this to our clients if it feels appropriate). The afflictions we may be suffering from can thus be seen in a very positive light. No longer do we just have to grin and bear our problems. We can actually do something very real to help ourselves by examining where or how the energy has become constricted, by looking at our underlying attitudes, and by developing a more peaceful state of mind. Once we have begun to see why we are sick, the road to health becomes apparent. Dis-ease, on any level, and to any degree, can be the most positive thing that could happen, as it gives us the opportunity for growth.

RECURRENCE

If the stress, or cause of the physical problem, is extremely deep-rooted, then there can be a recurrence of the problem some time after healing treatments have seemingly resolved the issue. This is due to attitude. The energy has been freed, a healing has taken place, but a repetition of stress can create the problem over again. It may be that through a fear that the condition will recur, that very fear re-creates it; or may be that the condition was so ingrained that there is a sense of loss without it. How often have we seen someone who lives in fear of developing an illness and then gets it? The fear creates stress, the stress leads to dis-ease.

So although a treatment can be effective, it is only the agent. The client is the one who has to generate the healing process itself. Easing the physical condition and feeling better is not the whole picture. We have to go on and change the patterns of our life, change our attitude, so that health becomes a normal and natural condition. Maintaining health and vitality depends upon us integrating a positive approach into our entire being, not just paying lip-service to it. Stress is caused by the deeper, more subtle aspects of our nature, as well as our surface thoughts. So we may act, and even think, we are being very positive, when deep inside there is still doubt and anxiety lurking.

Being in a state of ease demands great honesty. We are the only ones who will suffer if we ignore our inner fears and pretend everything is wonderful. It is very natural to be like this, for few of us are willing to expose ourselves as worried, guilty, or frightened. We want everyone to think we are strong, loving and confident, to the point where we almost believe it ourselves! It is when we fall sick again that our body reminds us of our deception.

Patterns of behaviour will constantly repeat themselves in our life until we see what the underlying meaning of them is. Many of us are familiar with this. We watch ourselves going from one disastrous relationship to another; we get sick regularly at the same time each year; we find ourselves constantly moving house; headaches always occur following particular events; or we may even go to numerous therapists, only to find nothing really changes. The same will happen if we have any form of healing (orthodox or alternative) but are not also open to changing within. As no one else inflicts sickness upon us, so no one else can take it away. The external can be soothed, but the internal will remain in turmoil if we are unable to be honest about our patterns, our fears, or our frustrations.

Physical dis-orders do not necessarily recur in the same form as before, so it is not always obvious that they have the same cause. For instance, a pain may develop in a particular area that pertains to the function of that area and where a related attitude has caused a physical weakness. Through healing, that weakness is strengthened, the attitude resolved, and the pain is free to go. A recurrence of the underlying cause will then find an outlet in another area of the body which reflects a similar or associated function and attitude. The cause is the same but we rarely recognise it as such because we fail to see the relationship between mind and body. Once we have changed our attitude, or recognised the cause, or integrated relaxation techniques into our life, then our body will no longer be subject to the hampering effect of stress. And when we do get sick we will see it as a direct message to examine our self and our way of life more deeply.

Skin problems are a perfect example of this. Teenagers suffer most from a lack of confidence, self-dislike, anger, and rebellion, caught between the dependent child and the independent adult. Acne expresses this through eruptions (anger and insecurity erupting) causing disfigurement (furthering self-dislike) and needing care and attention (like a child). Acne can also be caused by eating too much junk food which in turn affects the liver. The liver reflects our desire to live and is where we harbour fear and anger. Acne emerges mainly on the face as this part of us 'faces' the world. As the teenager matures, becomes more confident and able to cope with life, so this disturbed energy disperses.

Skin conditions later in life can thus indicate similar qualities as yet unresolved: feelings of inadequacy, of not being good enough, of being unloved or unwanted, of anger, particularly at the world for not giving fair dues. Skin disturbances other than acne, like excema, where it may cover the whole body, indicate this state to the point of being an allergy to the world, a 'keep clear' warning. The sadness of such problems is that the underlying message throughout is one of needing and wanting love, but the expression is one of anger or dislike that makes love back away. Yet until we can really love ourselves we will not be able to love others, and therefore let them love us. When we can love ourselves and begin to heal from the inside, then we find love being attracted to us.

In a healing treatment skin eruptions are seen to quieten, the rawness becomes calm and can soon dry up. This happens at the same time as the client is receiving channelled energy, a direct expression of love. That love soothes the conflict and inner pain. The nervous system relaxes, the blood is cleansed. The healing takes place because the client is re-energised with self-respect, confidence, and acceptance.

HEALING

The healing process itself can thus be seen as one that takes place within, through a release of the cause. Stress is an overall term we use to portray the various causes of dis-ease; healing is a bringing about of ease. To examine this further, let us look at some case histories that explore different aspects of the healing process.

The feeling of relaxation during a treatment that then brings the deeper release of stress can best be seen in the following quote, written by a client who came for a treatment feeling sceptical and doubtful that it could work:

> I had heard of channelled healing for many years and had fluctuating feelings about whether to believe in it or not. A friend of mine made an appointment for me, knowing I had two serious problems that the medical profession had been unable to help. I went feeling doubtful, but found that doubt disappearing about three minutes after she (the practitioner) began working on me. I slowly felt myself opening up, I perceived a profound trust, I felt relaxed, my fears vanished, and a warmth like the sun on a cold day ... Slowly a gentle tugging or pulling became very apparent. I

was feeling it in my neck but visualising it in my mind. It was like fingers moving the tissue, sorting it out, releasing it. I say 'fingers' for want of a better word, an area of energy perhaps, definitely there, working on my neck ... I could feel my organs moving. My large and small intestines were moving air and food through them. My lower pelvic area was stirring as though there was much blood and energy around ... I've also felt that my self-confidence and general well-being have been improved. I don't feel so scattered or lifeless as I did before.

Overcoming doubt and religious convention that channelled healing can work is not easy. One client said:

A few days before my appointment I struggled with a bit of doubt as to how open I could be to this kind of healing. The fundamental religion I was brought up with has us forever only "looking up" to God for healing, and has little acknowledgement of human beings' ability to be a channel and administer healing here and now ... However I am greatly relieved ... Due to a back injury I am normally aware of having to breathe deeper to ease tensions, for as a rule I breathe very shallowly. Near the end of the session I began to breathe easily without having to tell myself to do it. When I got up to leave I was aware that my spine was straight.

A mental and emotional healing was more prominent for a TV interviewer, Sarah. She came because of sleepless nights and digestive disorders. As a result of treatments she said:

I feel more relaxed and calm, and have a lighter feeling in my head. During a recent TV show, I consciously knew I was thinking before speaking, rather than blurting out whatever came into my mouth. This has been a major area of contention between my husband and I. It feels deeply satisfying to my being to know that areas I have been working on for months are now beginning to change, even on the emotional level.

Another aspect of emotional healing concerned Mary. There were very deep-rooted issues to do with her relationship with her father who had been dead for ten years, and she asked that the healing session help her deal with these:

What occurred during that treatment went very deep ... I was released from my negative feelings to do with him and with that gone I experienced an avalanche, a panorama of symbols of unity. Creativity was released. Light permeated my body and I was opened to my parents' love. It felt like a warm blanket around me. The verses of hymns that I had learnt as a child came flooding into my mind.

Taking responsibility for ourselves and putting that into action was seen in Barry, who was in his late 30s. He was slowy killing himself through drink and depression and his life energy was at a very low ebb, despite being a successful lawyer. When he came for a treatment it was obvious that he was heading for a major heart attack. He realised that he could choose whether to live or die, and in the moment of that realisation, Barry decided to live and started taking responsibility for himself. Within a few months, continuing with regular treatments, he had further explored his state of mind and begun to reverse his progression towards irreparable damage. He saw how his mind had stimulated his physical state and how his shift in attitude was now being reflected throughout his whole being.

A different aspect, that of absolute faith in the process, came with the case of John. He was a prisoner, out on parole. While in prison he had been suffering from severe abdominal pains and felt he might die when he returned to prison. He was convinced that his one healing treatment would be his cure. However, in the weeks following the treatment, nothing happened. He went back into prison saddened, yet still hoping that something would change. Three weeks to the day after the treatment he woke up without any pain, and has had no recurrences. He had almost lost hope as his expectations had been so high. But he didn't lose hope altogether. The three week interval was what his body had needed to integrate the energy and put the healing into operation. His persistent belief that he would recover eventually gave him the impetus to complete the process.

Occasionally the unexpected can happen. A client, Anne, came complaining of constipation. As the practitioner was short of time she worked only on the stomach and lower back areas, whereas normally she would have treated the whole body. The treatment was soon followed by a tremendous elimination. However, that night Anne was doubled up in pain, to the point where she was rushed to hospital. What she had not told the practitioner was that she had an enormous kidney stone, filling over half her kidney. The only means of removing this stone was through an operation. Now it became a different story as X-rays showed that the stone had begun to break up into small pieces and was dissolving. The pain she was experiencing was one particularly large piece travelling down the urethra. The treatment for constipation had seemingly given Anne the energy needed to also deal with this more serious difficulty.

Treatments are not limited to humans. Wherever there is life there can be a transference of energy for healing. One such example of this was that of a cat, Honey, who had feline leukaemia when she was nine months old. She recovered from this, but her owner was told that 95% of cats suffering in this way will die within a few years. When Honey was four years old she became seriously ill again, rapidly losing weight and strength. She was taken for a healing treatment. Following this she spent four days in a dark place, drinking occasionally but eating nothing. For the next three days she was taken out into the sunlight for a few hours each day, but still refused to eat. Late on the seventh night her owner was

41

awakened by a frightful screeching sound. The dehydrated and starving cat was now demanding food. Within another three days she had recovered her weight and vitality. The vet who had seen her and had held no hope whatsoever for a recovery, was astonished. Honey had followed her instinct to stay in the dark and to fast. The healing treatment had given her enough energy not only to do this, but also to heal herself effectively.

These examples show how varied the response to a treatment can be. When we are dealing with the cause, and not the symptom, it is not possible to predict what might happen. Illness, on any level, simply reflects energy that has become blocked, is being hindered in its flow and is therefore creating physical disorder. Wellness reflects the free movement of energy, whereby it can flow without difficulty. Although a symptom shows us there is an imbalance, it does not necessarily show us where that imbalance is, nor why it is there. And it need not be our concern. When we channel energy we are putting our trust in the energy to do the work necessary, there is no need to direct it purposefully or try to do anything. A restoring of harmony will take place in its own time and in its own way.

·4·
THE PRACTICE

This chapter outlines in detail what you need to know to be able to practise channelled healing. Practice makes perfect; without it you cannot move from who you are to who you can be. After a while you will find that you are practising twenty-four hours a day, that it has become ingrained into your being and is not something special that you do now and then. It becomes a way of life. Relaxation, meditation, attitude, openness, touching, healing, laughing – they all merge together and simply become an expression of one's beingness. So although this guide is essential for learning and developing an understanding, remember too that it is just a guide – eventually your own intuition and understanding will speak to you.

SETTING UP

Try to find a room to use that is not needed for other activities. In this way the atmosphere will grow, the room itself will be quiet and you will be able to tune into the quietness within yourself more easily. If a separate room is not possible, try to limit the activities that take place there. For instance, noisy children, television, or cigarette smoke can change the atmosphere in a room very quickly.

However, there can also be many times when you are working away from home and treating people in different environments, such as in hospital. So it is important not to place too much emphasis on always using the same space, or to get attached to the atmosphere in your room, or you will feel lost if you are not working there. Some people say that they can only channel if they are in a special place, that they must have these surroundings in order to be in tune with the divine. That is not the approach we recommend. Channelling energy is only dependent on the channel, the practitioner, not on the external environment. It can be done anywhere, at any time, if the practitioner is relaxed, confident and at peace. The divine is everywhere as it is always within us – it does not limit itself to certain places! Discovering the quiet within means that we are in touch with the divine at all times.

In the room that is used, check that there are no dead flowers or other signs of decay. Preferably have fresh flowers, plants, or a view over nature. This is simply to give inspiration through the involvement with life and growth.

Have a soft light. A bright light obviously makes it difficult for the client to relax, while a candle not only makes it difficult to see, but also creates an "esoteric" feeling which can be very off-putting to some people. A soft light, or perferably daylight, is appropriate.

There is no need to create a special atmosphere. Incense or music can be very distracting to clients. Some people find incense smoke very irritating – it can cause unnecessary coughing or sneezing, and we all have different tastes in music. So rather than cause further dis-ease, it is better to keep your room as simple and unpretentious as possible.

A chair will be needed for your client to sit on, preferably a straight-backed wooden chair that gives you plenty of access space. You will also need a table for the client to lie on. A massage table is ideal, or a wooden table of the same size, with a blanket or other padding on it. Cover this with a fresh clean sheet and a tissue for the head. The tissue should be changed after each client.

Obviously the room needs to be warm, but not too hot.

Your client will be relaxing but will be clothed and so will not lose much body heat. If it is too hot then the client will not be the only one falling asleep!

If there is a second room in the house or place of work that can be used, then after a treatment the client can be given time to rest there if needed, before leaving.

PERSONAL ATTITUDE

In order to channel energy it is important that you can free yourself of personal concerns. Take at least ten minutes at the beginning of each day to centre, relax, meditate, and focus within, to quieten the mind. It is not necessary to do this before each client, just once a day is sufficient. But you can judge this for yourself. If you find you are getting distracted or confused, or that your mind is chattering away, then take time out and become quiet again.

It is helpful not to eat too much while working. A full stomach demands a lot of energy to digest and will make you sleepy. You will be able to keep your energy at an optimum level by eating little.

It is essential that you feel peaceful, confident, and cheerful.

HOW LONG? HOW OFTEN?

The whole treatment should take no more than forty-five minutes, from when the client enters the room to when he leaves. This should include any talking at the beginning or end of the session, so the actual treatment is only thirty minutes long.

It is best not to try to fit too many people into one day, especially at the beginning. As you get more experienced, you will know your own limitations. Generally two people in the morning and two in the afternoon is enough. If this is too depleting then you can reduce the number of clients until

45

you feel comfortable. Give yourself a little time between people. If you book appointments on the hour, that should give you fifteen minutes between each one.

As you become known clients can begin to make demands, wanting to see you at difficult or inconvenient times. It is important not to let clients take advantage of you. If it is inconvenient to see them then say so. It is essential that you look after yourself as much as other people. If you respond to every request and do not pay attention to your own needs, then you will soon be exhausted, resentful, and unable to help anyone.

The number of treatments needed is not determinable in advance. The more treatments, the deeper the effect, but one, or only a few, may have already eased the problem. It is not in your authority as the practitioner to "prescribe" a certain number of treatments. However, if the complaint is serious you can recommend that a client comes on a regular basis, once a week, maybe twice in extreme cases, for three to four weeks. After this the treatments can be spread out to once every two weeks, then every three weeks, etc. Experience will teach you what is needed. Many clients come just when they want to and although you may recommend they come more often if you feel they need to, the choice will always be theirs.

Just as we avoid taking responsibility for ourselves and want someone else to heal us as quickly as possible, so you may find your clients asking for a lot of treatments. But increasing the treatments does not necessarily speed up the healing. Once the body has absorbed the energy it needs, it will not absorb any more, even if the treatment continues. There is a natural rhythm to healing that needs to be respected. You may also see clients going from one healing practitioner to another, even in the same day, in misguided hope that this will increase their rate of recovery. Looking inward and relaxing would be far more beneficial.

Receiving channelled healing treatments from more

than one practitioner in the same day can, in fact, create greater confusion. Each practitioner will be "in tune" in their own way and clients should be advised to stay with just one for at least a period of time. Forms of treatment other than direct hands-on healing will not interfere with the process, i.e. counselling or acupuncture. It has also been known for two or more practitioners to work on a client at the same time. The idea of group healing sessions is quite common but actually not very helpful. The energies become too conflicting for the body to deal with them effectively.

How often a treatment should be given may also depend on the state of the client's blood. Because of high levels of stress and the resulting dis-ease in the physical system, practitioners invariably find that the blood is the most contaminated part of the body. Accumulated stress releases toxins into the blood stream and this has to be cleansed and toned before further healing can take place.* While the treatments are continuing, further waste products will be released into the blood. For instance, as arthritis or similar conditions diminish, so the crystals formed by such afflictions will go into the blood stream to be removed. The blood therefore needs to be clean enough to deal with this.

STARTING

When an appointment is made, ask the client not to eat for at least one hour before coming, or if eating is necessary, to eat just a little. Before starting always make sure your hands are clean and free of odours, and that you look presentable. When a client comes, greet him with a cheerful smile to help

---

*Herbs can be used to aid the cleansing process. Those that are recommended for blood cleansing are: burdock root, dandelion, yellow dock, red clover, chapparral, and chlorophyll. They can be bought in capsule form or loose, from which a tea can be made. Up to five different herbs can be used in each tea, which should be drunk three times a day, preferably half to one hour before meals. Increased urination is to be expected as these herbs will also work as a diuretic.

him feel at ease and to convey the fact that this is not going to be an esoteric or strange experience.

Sit him in the chair and ask: "Why have you come to see me?" Relating his difficulties, whether they be physical, mental, emotional, or if he has come to simply experience the treatment, does not matter to you. But it gives him time to relax and feel at ease, and you time to attune to his energy. However, make sure that it does not go on for too long! Keep it to a minimum, or the appointment time will pass with the explanation. Many people need a sympathetic ear so they can release their problems. This is not necessarily your role, unless you wish to have two-hour-long appointments!

Before starting, explain clearly what you are going to do. This way your client will know what to expect and he will be able to relax. Without an explanation he will be wondering what is happening and so remain tense and uncertain, which is obviously what you wish to avoid. Explain to your client that you will first treat him sitting in the chair. He will then be asked to move to the table and to lie down, first on his back and then on his stomach. If he feels drowsy when he comes to lie down, he should not fight it but allow himself to go with it, even if he should fall asleep. Explain that you will be touching him quite lightly, starting at the head. Ask him to remove eye-glasses and shoes, and to take out any bulky objects from his pockets.

THE PRACTICE

When learning the different positions of the hands, it is advisable that they be held flat against the body as shown in Position (a), and not as shown in Position (b). This way, the hands will cover more of the body at once.

1.   Stand behind your client who is seated in the chair. Ask him to close his eyes as it will help him feel at ease. Rest your fingers very lightly on his shoulders for a few minutes. (Fig. 1). This allows your energies to blend, and gives you time to

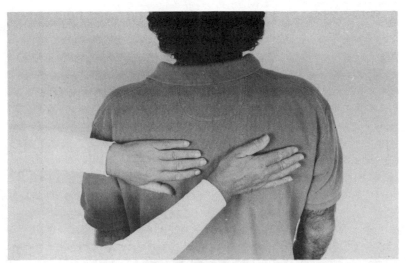

Position A

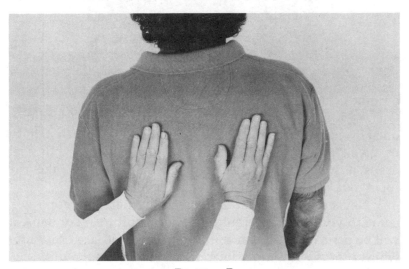

Position B

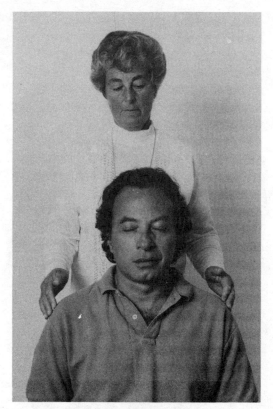

Figure 1

become centred and at peace.

As your client is now sitting quietly, gently ask him to open his heart and mind to the divine, and to ask for help to be given to his mental, emotional, spiritual, or physical needs, as well as to any specific problems. This now takes the focus away from you on a personal level.

Never stipulate what God or the divine is, as people will come to you from different beliefs and cultures. For some it will be perceived as great light or energy, the sun or nature, whilst others will simply look within their own hearts.

In every posture from now on, stay for 1½-2 minutes,

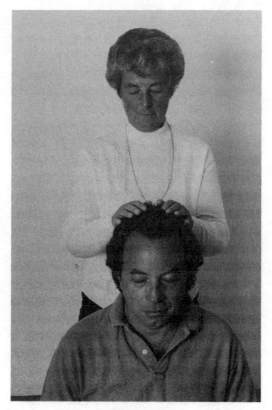

Figure 2

unless otherwise stated; if it is a problematic area then you
can stay for 3-4 minutes, or return after you have completed
the whole body. Always keep your hands very light – do not
let them become heavy nor increase the pressure.

2.   Bring your hands, palms down, very lightly on top of
the head (Fig. 2). Stay in this posture for about four minutes.
This balances the left and right hemispheres of the brain and
brings about equilibrium. It will also relax your client,
helping him to become more receptive. It releases tension in
the head and any mental problems. From here messages will
be sent by the brain throughout the entire nervous system.

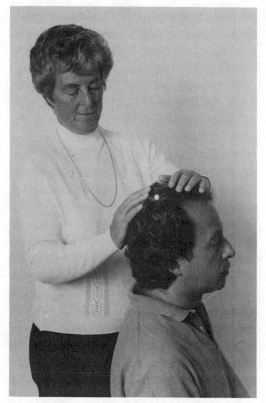

Figure 2(a)

3. Now move your hands and put one hand on top of the head and one hand at the back of the head (Fig. 2a).

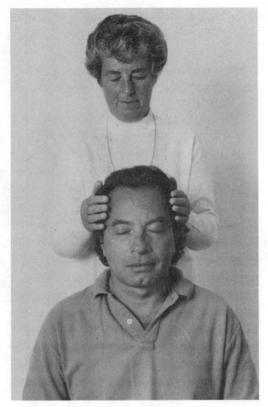

Figure 2(b)

4. Next, gently put your hands either side of the head, above the ears (Fig. 2b).

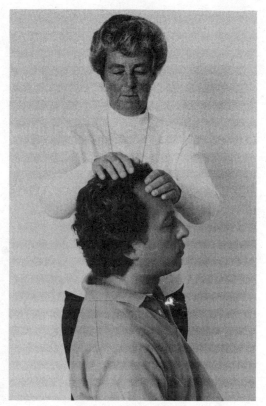

Figure 2(c)

5. Now move your hands and put one on top and one lightly over the forehead (Fig. 2c). This is stimulating the pineal and pituitary glands, which in turn instruct the other glands to provide the correct balance of hormones.

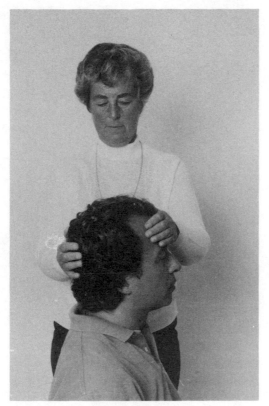

Figure 2(d)

6.   Your hands now move so you have one at the front and one at the back (Fig. 2d). This is working on creating a positive flow of energy in the mind.

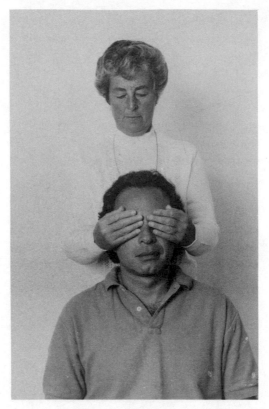

Figure 3

7.   Now bring your hands, palms inwards, very lightly over the eyes (Fig. 3).

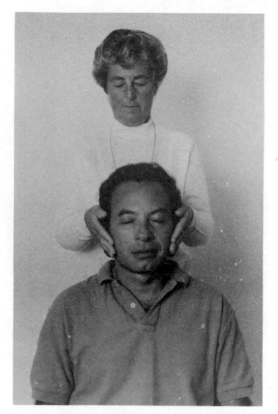

Figure 4

8. Do the same, bringing your hands over the ears (Fig. 4).

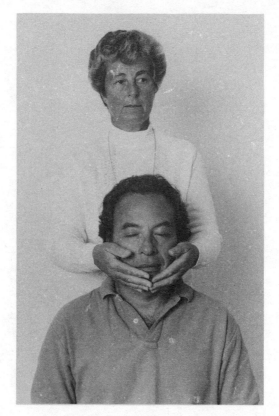

Figure 4(a)

9.   Put your hands over the jaw, mouth and teeth area, but only if it is problematic (Fig. 4a).

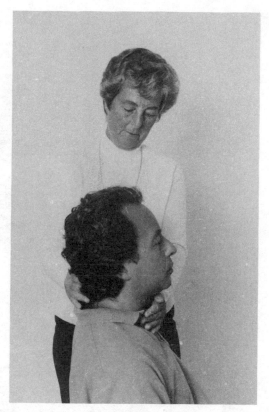

Figure 5

10. Next put one hand at the front of the throat and one hand at the back (Fig. 5). This stimulates the thyroid and parathyroid glands which control metabolism.

59

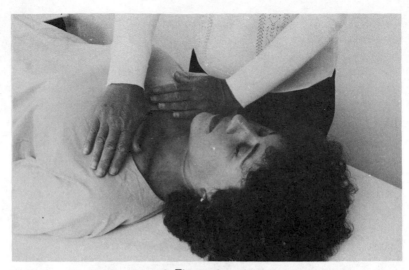

Figure 6

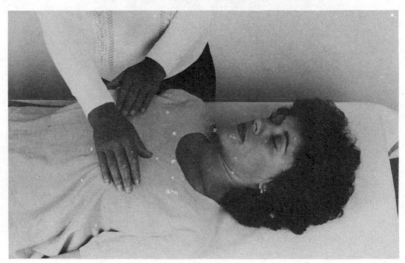

Figure 7

11. Now, in a quiet voice, ask your client to slowly lie down on his back on the table which has already been prepared, and to keep his eyes closed.

12. Lightly rest your hands on the top part of his chest (Fig. 6), over the collar bones. This clears congestion and breathing problems.

13. Move your hands down over the chest area (Fig. 7). For women, in this position, keep your hands 1½-2″ above the breasts, so as to avoid discomfort, stimulation, or embarrassment. This relaxes and can release tension nodules and breast problems.

14. Now put one hand over the spleen and one hand over the liver (Fig. 8). This energises these organs. If more heat is felt in either one of these, then bring both hands to that organ (Fig. 8a).

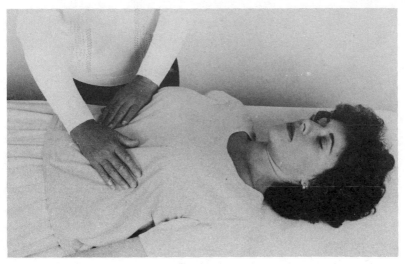

Figure 8

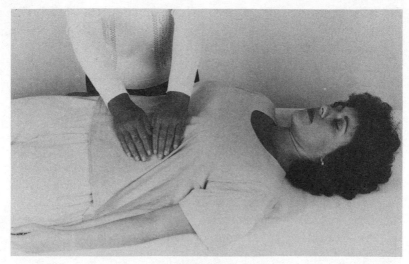

Figure 8(a)

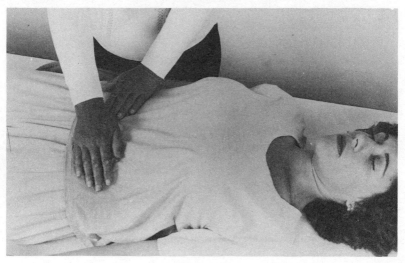

Figure 9

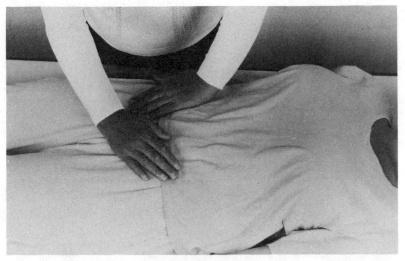

Figure 10

15.   Next put your hands on the front of the waist, covering the upper colon, and thereby releasing tension in the digestive system (Fig. 9).

16.   Your hands now move to the pelvis and small intestine area, covering the ovaries, prostate etc. (Fig. 10). These areas will become more relaxed and energised. In men this position is slightly lower than in women. To avoid stimulation, keep the hands 1½-2″ above the body.

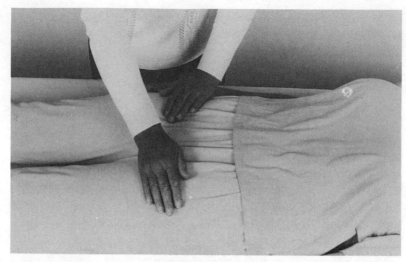

Figure 11

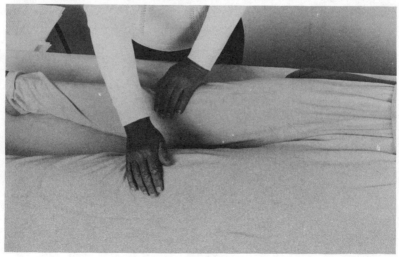

Figure 11(a)

17.   Joints tend to become areas of stiffness and great pain.
The following positions greatly assist in the loosening and
release of this. Firstly put one hand on either upper thigh
(Fig. 11).

64

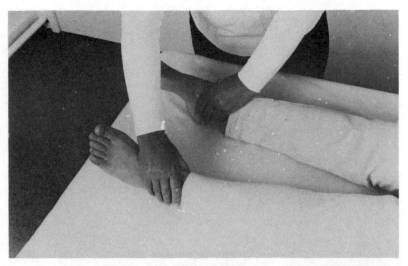

Figure 11(b)

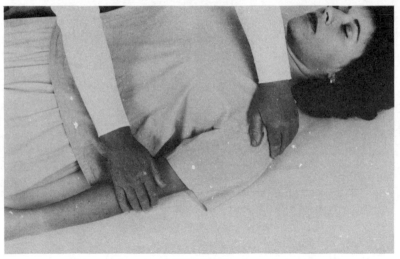

Figure 12

18. Move your hands down to cover the knees (Fig. 11a).
19. Now put your hands on the ankles (Fig. 11b).
20. Now move up and put one hand at the shoulder and put the other one at the elbow (Fig. 12).

65

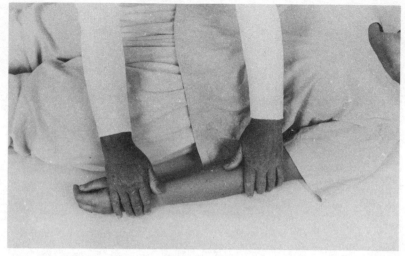

Figure 12(a)

21. Next move the hands down so the one from the shoulder moves to the elbow, and the one at the elbow moves to the wrist (Fig. 12a). Then make sweeping movements from the shoulder down over the hand and away. Do this two to three times. After this do the opposite shoulder and arm.

22. Ask your client to gently turn over so that he is lying on his front, keeping his eyes closed. Have his arms by his sides, his head turned to either the left or right.

23. Place one hand over the base of each foot (Fig. 13). In this position, energy will flow through the entire body.

24. Then put one hand resting lightly just on the nape of the neck and the other hand on the tailbone (Fig. 14). This is especially for those who are low in energy. As the spine contains the central nervous system, so from here, nerves reach out to different organs and areas of the body; as you work along the spine, these nerves become energised, and in turn energise and strengthen the organs and glands.

25. Keeping your upper hand still, bring the lower hand up over the buttocks (Fig. 14a).

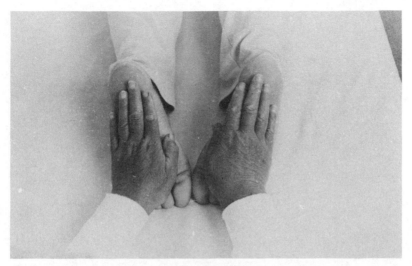

Figure 13

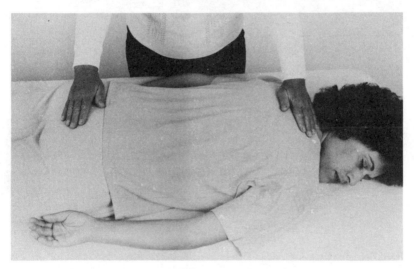

Figure 14

26.   Still keeping your upper hand in place, bring your lower hand up to the waist/middle area of the back (Fig. 14b).

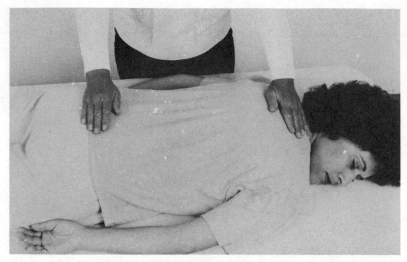

Figure 14(a)

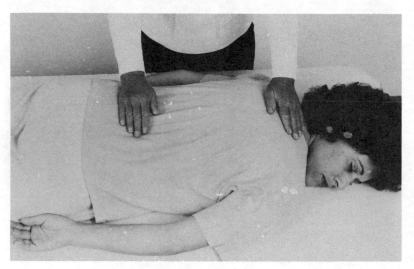

Figure 14(b)

27.   Now leave your lower hand in place and bring your upper hand down between the shoulder blades (over the heart area) (Fig. 14c).

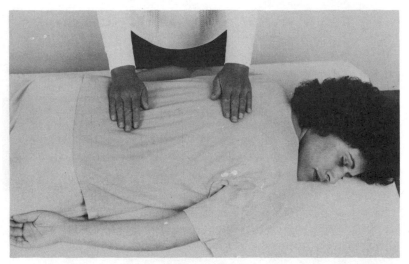

Figure 14(c)

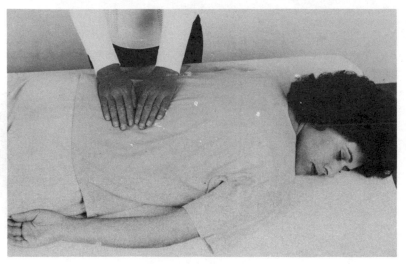

Figure 14(d)

28.   Now move both hands to be side by side in the middle of the back (Fig. 14d).

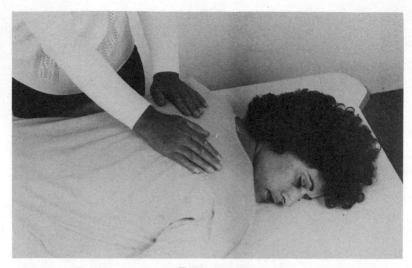

Figure 15

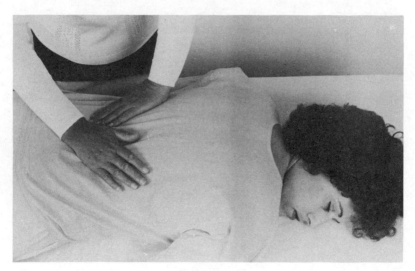

Figure 16

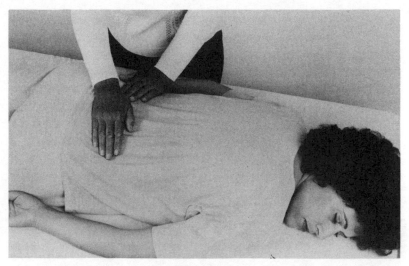

Figure 17

29. Next move your hands to cover the upper back area on each side (Fig. 15). This is especially for the lungs and nerves.
30. Next put one hand over each kidney, upon which sit the adrenal glands (Fig. 16). This energises that area.
31. Now move your hands down to just below the waist/upper lumbar region (Fig. 17). This is an extremely common area for lower back pain.

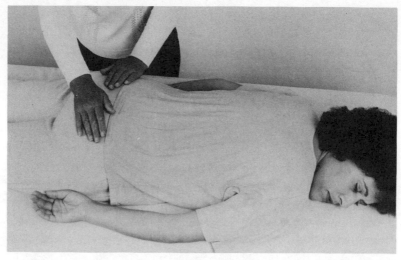

Figure 18

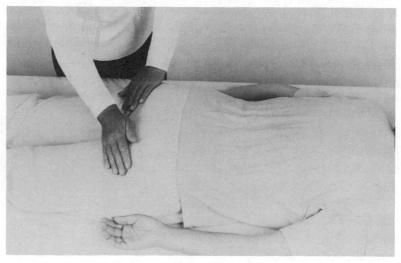

Figure 18(a)

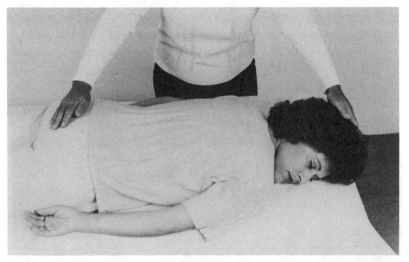

Figure 19

32.   Next move your hands over the buttocks in two movements. Firstly over the upper buttock and pelvis area (Fig. 18); secondly in the lower buttock area, slightly under the rise (Fig. 18a). This not only energises these areas, but is also important in treating the nerves throughout the pelvis, legs, back, intestines, and uterus.

33.   Now make slow sweeping movements from the buttocks down each leg and out over the feet. Do this two to three times. If there are specific problems in the legs then you can spend more time in the appropriate area. Do not work directly on varicose veins (see under "Treatments").

34.   Now put one hand at the crown of the head and one hand at the tailbone (Fig. 19). Stay here for two to three minutes. Energy will be flowing smoothly along the entire central nervous system.

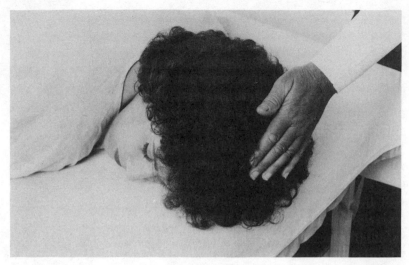

Figure 20

35.   Now leave one hand at the crown of the head and remove your other hand, letting it drop by your side (Fig. 20). Your attention is on the top of the head and you can mentally acknowledge that the treatment is now over, giving thanks for having been used as a channel.

TREATMENTS

Generally a treatment consists of doing the head, the rest of the body, and then some extra time may be spent on areas of specific need. By doing the whole body, any areas associated with the problem will also be eased. The return to the area of need, or a longer time spent there, gives extra energy, but always this is done in relation to the whole. This is the case even for problems in the head, i.e. eye problems are often associated with the kidneys and elimination. By doing the whole body this is eased, and the energy is then freed to work on the eyes.

However, there are specific needs that can arise where the treatment may differ slightly:

74

Accidents: No matter what the problem, always treat the head, as here the healing energy can be released and the shock eased. Then treat the head and the area damaged, with one hand on each. You can also treat the heart, for shock.

Twists and Sprains: Do the head for 5 minutes, then hold the twist or sprain between your hands for 10 minutes.

Fall: This creates shock so it is essential to do the head, spine, and also the heart, especially in older people.

Headaches: There are different types of headaches: 1. At the front of the head. This is usually caused through bad digestion, so apart from doing the head, also do the intestinal area. An elimination will help. 2. At the back and at the top of the head. This is usually caused by stress, or a constriction of the blood supply and therefore a lack of oxygen to the brain. Do the head and a few minutes over the whole body.

Varicose Veins: Do not touch the leg directly, as heat from your hands can damage the vein, as it is so near to the surface. Instead keep your hands $1\frac{1}{2}$-2" above the leg while you are working there.

Emotional or Psychological Crisis: Always do the head. Also in these cases it can help to do the heart and spleen, as there is a direct link between the head and these two organs.

FINISHING

After you have finished, let go and do not hold on to any of what has taken place. Release completely. Then quietly you can tell your client: "It's all finished, you can open your eyes now."

Washing your hands and wrists in cold water is important if you have been treating a serious illness, or the feet. It is also advisable to go to the toilet to get rid of any excess fluid which might have collected during the treatment.

When your client "comes to" he has usually experienced a wonderful feeling of well-being, but sometimes the need to lie down will come to him after he gets home. So always

75

suggest that if he can rest for a half hour or an hour then this will help. If he should fall asleep during this rest, then to sleep until he wakes. The healing proces will be continuing on a much deeper level during this time. If necessary, and if you have the room, he can rest before going home.

In some cases your client will already be sleeping before the treatment is over. Do not try to wake him, but every five minutes or so you can softly say: "It's OK now, I've finished, you can wake up." Ten to fifteen minutes is possible before a natural waking will usually occur.

After the treatment, before your client leaves, and if he is going by car, you can advise him to drive carefully as he may feel a little drowsy or light-headed.

If possible, now sit quietly for five minutes in a meditative state. It is extremely important that you do not get personally involved or caught up in your client's problems and difficulties. Having heard a story and given a treatment, it is surprising how affected you can be by whatever situation you have just dealt with. You have to let this go. You cannot help your clients by feeling sad for them. Compassion is more important. Send your compassion to them, then let them go. If you carry your clients with you, then you will soon drain your energy. You have done all you can do and it is no longer in your hands. It is better just to listen sympathetically and to allow the energy to move through you without obstruction, rather than getting involved with the difficulties. If you get involved, you will hinder the energy flow and will be of no help.

LEGALITY

If you intend to practise professionally, it is a good idea to check whatever laws there are in your country or state regarding touch. Some ask for massage licences, some do not. As you are working with your client fully clothed, it usually makes the requirements somewhat easier.

·5·
THE PRACTITIONER'S EXPERIENCE

As you are treating a client, you may find different sensations, feelings, images, or actions taking place within you. This is perfectly natural. You are channelling energy, allowing it to move through you, and as such you have become more open and sensitive to both yourself and others. You may find yourself tuning in without even realising it and experiencing many different manifestations of energy. As a general rule, let these experiences go. Take no notice of them. They are simply manifestations and not important in themselves. By concentrating on your work, on being quiet, anything experienced will be resolved. Paying attention to the experiences or thinking they are important signs of your power will actually hold you back from being an open channel.

HANDS LEAVING THE BODY

As you are working you may find that your hands move away from the body and appear to be working approximately 1½-2″ above. This is the energy field surrounding each person. (If your hands move more than 2″ away then you should bring them back.) You can let your hands be at this short distance (1½-2″) for as long as you want, before they naturally return to the body. There is the possibility of doing the entire treatment in this way, but let it develop in its own time. What needs to be done first is to develop your channelling abilities and the confidence to touch another person.

VIBRATIONS

This is very common. Your hands may vibrate, or pick up vibrations in your client. Do not pay undue attention to it at this point. Simply complete the position and move onto the next one. Pulsations or energy sensations under the hands can be experienced fairly often – you may even feel subtle movements, or a definite movement of the flesh or bone. Do not get alarmed. It is simply the rebalancing of energy taking place. Acknowledge, let go, and do not interfere.

IMPRESSIONS

Different images may come to you, including colours (especially violet or green); religious symbols; healing symbols; beautiful landscapes; or the organs of the body. You may even "see" the diseased parts of the body you are working on. Acknowledge but do not hold on to these images. They are simply a reflection of your openness.

You may also "hear" a voice or receive strong impressions or inner guidance telling you what is wrong with the person you are treating, the basic cause of the complaint, and how to help. You may also "know" when something has lessened or been healed. Use your judgement as to whether or not to tell the client what you have intuited.

Many practitioners become excessively interested in telling their client what is wrong with him, what they have "psychically" picked up. This focuses and limits the mind to the practitioner's version of what is wrong. It does not acknowledge the inner energy of the client as being the healing force. Although most clients like to know what is wrong, we need to ask ourselves if it is appropriate to tell them, especially if we trust the life energy as being able to rebalance without the need of labels, definitions or interpretations. At times it may be advisable to remain quiet and let the healing proceed in its own way, for a client does not have to know what is wrong in order to heal, whereas if he does know (or thinks he knows) it can create concern, confusion, or apprehension. Consequently, we do not necessarily achieve anything constructive by telling someone what we have intuited as the problem, except perhaps, for self-gratification at how psychic we are! It is not easy to be content with humility and a trust in the divine.

At other times, it may be clear that we should say something, that if the client knows more about his condition or how he can help himself, it will enable a deeper release. At all times, however, it is important to remember that it is not a diagnosis, simply the conveying of an impression. You are not a medical professional. If it sounds like a definite statement, it may not only cause alarm, but can also be misleading.

As you begin to learn about the healing process, you may "receive" all kinds of information that you do not fully comprehend, or that you misinterpret. For instance, you can be very aware that your client has a problem in the intestinal area, but out of inexperience you may convey this to your client as if it were cancer or something equally serious, thus causing intense concern. And it could be a very inaccurate translation of the problem. It would be better to calmly advise medical tests, without creating unnecessary worry. As your sensitivity increases and your understanding of what is taking place deepens, so you will be able to respond to your clients with greater tact, objectivity, and less urgency to share your "information". This is one area where it is extremely easy for the ego to get involved, so at all times a trust in the divine and in life itself will help balance this.

It is also important, if you do talk with your clients, to help them see their illnesses in a more positive way, to see that this is a time for change and growth. Illness is the indication of imbalance on inner levels, so it offers the chance to bring about a deeper state of balance than may have been realised was needed. From a naturopathic point of view, it is felt to be far more positive that the affliction is now manifesting, than staying locked inside. Practitioners can help their clients to grasp this attitude and therefore not to feel helpless or victimised by their difficulties.

SYMPTOM TRANSFERRAL

Picking up your client's pain or symptoms is very easy in the early stages. Do not get annoyed with yourself if this should happen. As you become more competent it will change. However, it is not pleasant to experience and a continual working in this way can drain your energy a great deal. Many people seem to think it is an indication of having special receptive powers, or as a sign of great healing abilities, but this is not so. It is more an indication of being attached to the situation, of being personally involved. And it is of no benefit to anyone.

If you find you are absorbing symptoms, then, after your client has gone, take time to yourself and sit quietly. Accept what has happened. Acknowledge that the pain being felt is not yours. It is a pain that you do not want and does not have anything to do with you. See it begin to leave. Feel the pain receding until it has diminished. It is not yours and you do not need it.

The picking up of symptoms is an important indication of your ability to be detached. Are you getting more involved than you thought? How clear is your motivation? Are you actually trying to heal, rather than just being an agent through which people can heal themselves? The more you can "step aside" and allow the energy to flow through you, the less you will be subject to picking up energy that then drains or confuses you.

HEADACHES AND EXHAUSTION

This comes from trying to do too much. The ability to channel is something that grows with time. Do not try to force the issue. Through experience you will get to know your own level of capability. There is no point in overdoing it, for you will not be able to help anyone that way. Looking after yourself is more important than thinking you can treat everyone who comes along. Pace it out, take time. Have a rest whenever needed. Exhaustion usually comes from a giving of your own energy, rather than from channelling energy, but nonetheless, learning and practising any new technique takes time.

A headache may be due to stress, tension, constipation, or a build up of toxins. Or it may be from trying too hard. Relax. Accept and love yourself as you are. Come back to the quiet within. There is nothing to force, nothing to try to do. The harder you try the less you will achieve. There is no need to worry if it doesn't happen as you want it to. Relaxing will help it far more than continuing to push yourself.

HOT/COLD/DENSE/FLUID

Sensations such as these are very normal. Temperatures, from hot to cold, will vary and change in different parts of the body. Areas may also feel dense, solid, hard to move through, while other areas may feel fluid, soft, easy to move in. Acknowledge and let go. Holding on to these images creates a personal involvement. They are simply areas of varying energy states and make no difference to the treatment you are giving. Some areas may also appear very dark, like a black cloud which tends to indicate a recent problem. Light patches indicate an older problem. This sort of information is simply received and then let go. It is not important.

HEAT AND PERSPIRATION

Getting hot and/or perspiring is a further sign of picking up energy. It is a reaction of the nervous system. Here again it is important to relax, become calm within, take deep breaths and let go. If you are at peace in yourself then you will not get caught up in energy manifestations. If you feel you are at peace, yet these sensations continue, then just let them be. You are open and receptive and sometimes such responses are unavoidable. It will clear very quickly if you do not pay any attention to it.

STAYING GROUNDED

Your clients will experience any number of feelings and thoughts during a treatment and may have the release of past traumas or difficulties. As you are the only one with them, you are also the one to whom they will turn. Obviously your detachment does not stop you from being a caring and compassionate listener. Offer whatever support feels appropriate at the time, remembering that your job is not that of therapist or physician. Give your clients space, allowing them the freedom to express themselves and the safety to do so, at the same time remaining centred and quiet within yourself. Know when a client may need to be alone and so do not urge him to talk. Recognise your personal limitations, whether that of time or experience, and stay clear in yourself. Many healing practitioners find it very beneficial also to train as a counsellor; it is important at least to feel confident within yourself that you can deal with the situation.

The process of healing is different for each person so nothing can ever be predicted. You may have clients experiencing great release, or just getting frustrated if their expectations of the treatment are not met, because they do not realise that healing is taking place, even if they cannot see or feel it. Trust yourself and trust the work and do not try to be something or someone you are not. Explain gently that the treatment is over and suggest they rest awhile either before leaving or when they get home. By staying quiet in yourself you will find you can deal with the situation much more easily than you might have thought. Staying grounded means staying clear in yourself and not getting caught up in, or taking on, other peoples' difficulties. By staying grounded you can allow the process to work without being affected.

·6·
THE CLIENT'S EXPERIENCE

As the client is receiving a treatment, all manner of different sensations may be experienced and the release of past traumas or difficulties may also take place. You need to appreciate these experiences and to be able to reassure your client that what is happening is quite normal.

RELAXATION

This is, naturally, the most gratifying experience. Clients may go into a very deep relaxation, sometimes sleep, or simply feel at peace, calmed of fears and worries. This peace can continue and a new sense of balance and harmony emerge. They may even go into a deep state of meditation. Be sensitive to this so that after the treatment is over, you do not disturb them too harshly.

Afterwards they invariably feel calmer and better able to cope with any difficulties. Eyes will be brighter, the face infused with colour, there will be more energy, and a joyful or confident attitude. All of this is due to the input of energy coming through the practitioner. That energy seeks out areas of stress and dis-ease, loosens blockages and increases the flow. The client's body then uses this energy to invigorate areas of need, relax constrictions, and to begin the healing process.

HOT/COLD

Changing of temperature in the body is very common. It can

vary from hot to cold, and may induce perspiration or shivering. This occurs as the energy is moving around the body, rebalancing. You can reassure your clients that this sensation will clear very soon.

Heat is usually an indication that unwanted toxins or emotions are being released into the blood, and an opening of joints or constrictions taking place. For instance, during a treatment for arthritis, rheumatism, or other such disorders, a client may experience tremendous heat coming from your hands. This heat enables an unlocking of the joints to take place, followed by a breaking down of the calcium deposits which are then removed by the blood.

Cold indicates circulation difficulties, sometimes due to bad digestion, which in turn is invariably due to stress. Stress also constricts the circulation. Shivering indicates a letting go of past fear or trauma, a "shaking off" effect, often unconscious. Deep sighs are another indication of this.

HEART VARIATIONS

The rhythm of the heart may change temporarily, either palpitating or slowing down. It will rebalance very quickly. It is simply indicating the movement of energy. Palpitations may indicate the release of inner fears or anxieties; a slowing down of the heart rate usually accompanies a state of deep relaxation or meditation.

MOVING ENERGY

Experiencing energy moving can be a little disconcerting, especially if it feels like "rushes" or waves passing through the body. Sometimes it may feel like a heavy weight pressing down. However, all this will balance very quickly.

Clients sometimes feel as if there were hands on their body other than your own. They may feel them in different parts of the body, in the same place as where you are working but increased, or even inside their body. This is the energy coming into them and working in the areas where it is needed. They may also experience vibrations coming from your hands. All of this is quite normal and will not continue after the treatment is over. Fleshy lumps or growths may be felt to dissolve or move, dispersing into the blood stream. This may not happen all at once – it could take quite a few sessions, but it is the result of the relaxation and ease circulating throughout the body.

TINGLING

This experience may vary from a slight tingling to a real electric shock type feeling, running down one part of the body or even all over. Congestion is being freed and the energy is moving again, opening passages that were previously blocked. As the energy moves, so it can be felt in this way.

PULLING

As if being pulled from the inside, or muscles gently tugged into a new position, this experience is an indication that the channelled energy is working on realignment.

PAIN

As energy flows back into constricted parts of the body, pain may be experienced. Generally this will not last for more than forty-eight hours at the most, and it is advisable to stay in bed or rest while this is happening. It occurs when the area has been "dead" or numb for a period of time, i.e. when a slipped disc begins to go back into place, the vertebrae will have to be realigned, as they have become accustomed to the damaged pattern. The area may be tender for a while until the more healthy pattern becomes established.

87

VISUALISATION

All sorts of images, visualisations, or "mystical" experiences may occur in the mind (similar to the practitioner's experience). These visualisations are entirely spontaneous and often very beautiful. They may manifest as clarity, light, or inner vision, a change in consciousness, or a new purpose in life. It is uplifting and revitalising, as new aspects of one's being become apparent, and can bring joyful weeping or laughter.

Another aspect of visualisation is one where the client can purposefully visualise areas of difficulty or pain in his body as recovering. This is especially supportive in cases of paralysis. The client can "see" the unused part of his body getting better, moving again, and gaining strength. The client can also talk and give verbal encouragement to his body; the message will be received by the brain and conveyed by the nervous system to the relevant area. It eases fear, worry, and confusion, and it is a way of developing love for oneself. It represents a change in attitude.

RELEASE

As the inner causes of the difficulties are loosened, so there can be the release of emotional or psychological trauma. This is not unusual and can vary from being a simple resolution of a past difficulty, to a letting go of deeper experiences. Long-held and repressed memories surface, in order to be resolved. These memories can be unpleasant, but that is why they are being released. They may include visions, sounds, or smells from the past; relationships with parents or siblings can be thrown into new light; pain, guilt, tension or anxiety, can be relived, but in that reliving there is a release, a final letting go. Often this form of release is essential before any physical progress can be made. The trauma not only caused the physical problem but is also perpetuating it. Once there has been personal resolution, then the ensuing freedom can enable the body to become free.

If your clients are in need of support, then you can reassure them that this release is a wonderful part of the healing process as it enables them to be free to move into whole new areas of their being. Without it the trauma stays repressed inside, causing further stress and dis-ease.

After a treatment, there can also be feelings of sadness, even depression. Clients should be warned that this may happen. This is because the release of deep-seated memories, thoughts, and feelings, is going on, even though they may not be fully experiencing it consciously. The release is essential. Years of carrying secret guilt, for instance, can lead to innumerable problems, particularly in the stomach or upper back, such as shoulder pain. The letting go of this guilt is like the dropping of a heavy burden which had become so familiar that a client may not even have noticed he was carrying it.

As stated before, whatever happens, simply support your clients in whatever way you feel you can. Trust the work. Do not try to be a counsellor. You are who you are. The letting go is an integral part of the healing process. Not all clients will experience it of course; and some will do so only after they have left you and are alone again.

Integrating these experiences happens naturally, as the release has. There is a moving on, beyond the experience, to new areas. However, that integration is also somewhat dependent on how a client continues with his life. If after having had a treatment, he goes on with an unaware lifestyle, not watching his diet, not relaxing, or taking time to look within, then it is possible that traumas and illnesses will recur. There is no point in being dependent on a healing practitioner in order to stay healthy. Clients have to take responsibility for their own state of health. Relaxation and meditation are not just for the practitioner but for the clients as well!

MEDICAL FOLLOW-UP

For clients wishing to have X-rays after a treatment, it is advisable for them to wait about one or two weeks. In this way integration will have fully taken place. Nothing may be visible if X-rays are taken within twenty-four hours of a treatment. The body needs time to integrate the energy and begin to make changes.

This also applies to any other medical checks or tests that may be applicable. If done too soon, the client may feel let down and that nothing has actually happened. A time for integration is essential.

CHOOSING A PRACTITIONER

As important as it is for practitioners to be honest in their dealings and treatments of clients, so it is for the client to be honest about his feelings. When a client comes to a practitioner he has to really want this particular person to work with him, or there will be a resistance to receiving. A practitioner should look positive, healthy, disciplined, and at peace – a sense of inner ease is vital.

Too often, when we visit a medical doctor, we feel inferior and that we are somehow at fault; there is no sense of ease, and we may also feel that we have no choice. In this work, the client's trust and confidence in the healing practitioner is essential – without it there can be no relaxation or release of stress, and the client will come away equally troubled as when he arrived. And there can be choice. The choosing of a practitioner is an expression of the desire to change, it is the taking of responsibility; it is the selection of those with whom one wishes to share the change.

·7·
GOING FURTHER

As we practise and develop our understanding of the healing process, it becomes obvious that there is far more going on than we may ever really know. A human being is a complexity of thoughts, feelings, urges, instincts, impulses, memories, tissues, organs, bones, blood, chemicals, cells, hormones, flesh, breath, and, pervading all, the unseen elements of energy and spirit. Not only can we not hope to understand this magnificent creature in its entirety, but there is no need to do so. It understands itself very well indeed and better so without our interference. When we do interfere with the natural functioning of this being by imposing unhealthy or stressful patterns of behaviour, so we create an imbalance, and the normally smooth functioning mechanism begins to break down.

A deeper understanding of energy patterns and the manifestations of imbalance can enable us to maintain a greater degree of health. In learning about the healing process, it can therefore be very beneficial to explore the different types of healing therapy available and to appreciate how they work. It may not make any difference to our actual practice but it can broaden the basis from which we work and open us to furthering our comprehension of what being human is all about.

Life is here to be discovered. At present man uses only about 10 per cent of his brain capacity. There are vast, uncharted areas within us lying dormant that we know little or nothing about. In other words, we are capable of far more than we think we are. We can delve deeper and explore further these unknown realms awaiting us, and each new learning experience will open us that much more to the wonders of man, to the extraordinary powers we really possess, and to the great potential within us all. Much of this becomes clearer as we practice meditation and focus our minds, or when we go into deep relaxation and the internal chatter begins to recede. It is here that we can release the need to interfere, and can surrender to the stillness.

As we explore further in this way, it soon becomes obvious that we create our own obstacles; that due to looking at everything with a subjective, self-centred attitude, so we hold ourselves back from further growth. But selflessness is not an act of negation – we do not have to overcome our ego, or deny it, or somehow get rid of it. Rather, we reach a point where the ego's demands and involvement become obsolete, unnecessary, and we can go beyond them. It is a process that takes place as we move from individualism to compassion, from arrogance to humility, from ignorance to understanding. We begin to put our own desires out of business as our focus becomes that of the divine.

We do not have to try to do something specific to achieve this. If we try to do something it indicates a lack of peace with our present condition and a lack of trust in the process. Trying to do something is not the doing of it. Not trying is a state of being totally here and now in the present moment. It is a dropping away of the superfluous, the games, the personal trips, the need for reassurance or gratification. It is a state of basic sanity. We are who we are, here and now, without any preconceived ideas of ourself.

Religion or philosophical systems of thought can aid us in this development, as they encourage us to look deeper within ourselves. Man's purpose on the highest level is to achieve oneness with the divine, whereby the personal self or ego no longer plays any part. Religion and philsophy offer us different guidelines or maps to reaching this state and all are valid. No one way can ever be right for everyone, nor complete in its explanation, for words can never fully explain the unexplainable.

There are many paths up a mountain. They will all get us there, but no one path is the only way to go. Each of us has to find our own way. There are signposts that can point us in the right direction but it is we who have to climb the rocks, cut down the jungle, or traverse the chasms. Exploring the various maps as we go is a way of getting to know our terrain. We can be warned of some of the pitfalls that lie ahead, aided when we fall into difficulty, and gently steered back on course when we lose direction. Understanding our mountain and what it is made of, reading the guidelines those who have gone before us have left, and learning to identify the signs along the way, all help our journey to be a smoother one.

No one else can do this for us, we are the only ones who can deal with our selfish desires, our confusion or our hopelessness. There is a tendency to believe that some great external experience will somehow change us, will transform our consciousness, and we may spend years chasing after this ultimate experience. But the only way to really discover the unseen and the unknown is through the diligence of meditation or contemplation. It is here that the freedom from that which holds us back is found. The mountain that has to be climbed is inside us.

It is rarely a clear journey or even an easy one. Again and again we find ourselves working blind, with the faith that the purpose is being fulfilled, that integration is taking place even when there appears to be disintegration. Being blind demands total trust in the life force that it is doing what is right for us. [8]

There are many new systems and paths emerging and an equal number of masters proclaiming the way. Knowing who to trust, who is right or wrong, can be confusing. The Buddha offered some extremely useful advice when he told his monks not to take anything he said as true until they had experienced it for themselves. When it had become a living reality, then they could know what was the truth and what was not, for themselves, and not just because he had told them.

Trusting our intuition in this regard is essential. If there is any doubt about a particular method or teacher, then we should question and probe until we feel clear in ourselves. One safe guideline to follow is that where there is tradition or lineage (the passing on of teachings from master to disciple through the ages) then we can know that the methods have been tried and tested many times over, and can therefore be relied upon as safe and effective. Where there is no history, when the methods being taught have only recently been developed, then there are no guarantees, there is no way of knowing what the long term benefits or risks may be. We can also ask ourselves if we see very basic qualities being developed, such as humility, grace, or unconditional love. Or if instead, the emphasis lies on developing self-centred qualities such as personal power, mastership over others, or coveted wealth. Does the method encourage service to others, or the exploitation of others? The ego is very deceptive and instead of finding a way to go beyond it, we can very often actually find ourselves getting immersed in it even more.

Out of the philosophical traditions of the past that have developed through thousands of years of experience, has come a fully comprehensive understanding of man, the relationship between mind and body, and how to integrate this knowledge. Healing through touch is a part of this tradition, as it is based on love and humility. We find accounts of it not only in Christianity, but also in many of the religions of the East. A healthy mind is essential for deeper spiritual progress, and a healthy body is interdependent with a healthy mind. We find descriptions of different healing techniques (acupuncture, acupressure, reflexology, massage); nutritional guidelines (naturopathy, the use of herbs); physical exercises (hatha yoga, t'ai chi); breathing techniques; the use of colour; relaxation; purification and cleansing techniques; and detailed teachings on the energy centres within us (Chakras). Exploring all of this takes far more time than we can devote here, but at least a basic understanding is recommended.

THE CHAKRAS

Within our body there are seven principle centres of energy known as chakras. These are situated over or very close to the glands of the endocrine system and to major nerve plexuses, intersecting the spine at certain points. They have been known in ancient texts as the Seven Seals or the Seven Sacred Glands. The word chakra is actually of Hindu origin, literally meaning "wheel of fire". Yoga developed specific ways (such as asanas and breathing techniques) to stimulate these chakras, and also visualised them as open lotus blossoms.

The first chakra, "Mooladhara", means the root centre. It is connected to the coccyx and is actually between the urinary and excretory orifices. It is associated with our potential as human beings, to basic survival needs, and the more primitive or instinctive aspects of our nature.

The second chakra, "Swadhisthana", means "one's own abode". It intersects the spine at the first lumbar and is connected to the spleen and pancreas. It is associated with the unconscious, with sexual urges and base relationships.

The third chakra, "Manipura", means the "city of jewels". It is at the eighth thorax and is connected to the solar plexus and adrenals. It is associated with power, self-centred emotion, and self-identification.

The fourth chakra, "Anahata", which literally means

"unstruck", but is otherwise known as the heart chakra, situated at the first thorax, near the thymus gland. It is associated with compassion, love, and affection.

The fifth chakra, "Vishuddhi", means to purify. It is at the throat, intersecting the third cervical near the thyroid. It has to do with communication, expression, and higher thought processes.

The sixth chakra, "Ajna", is known as the third eye chakra, located between the eyebrows and connected to the first atlas bone and the pituitary gland. It has to do with self-awareness on a higher level, inner vision, bliss, joy, and the power of the mind.

The seventh chakra, "Sahasrara", is more than just a chakra, as it is at the crown of the head and is associated with the pineal gland. It represents the seat of self-realisation, the highest consciousness or enlightenment.

The chakras relate to the physical, emotional, mental, and spiritual aspects of our being, directly connecting our mind and body. In most people they remain closed or functioning in only a minimal way. As we develop consciously they begin to open, and thus enable us to reach higher levels of consciousness.

Our development moves upward through these chakras. Generally mankind operates from the second chakra, through a gratification of desires; political leaders operate from the third, in expressing the instinct for power; the sages and more developed teachers see the world through the fourth chakra, that of love and compassion. As we evolve in consciousness, so our understanding deepens. From a lower level it is difficult to understand the higher levels; as we open the higher levels we not only see the lower ones more clearly, having once been there ourselves, but our experience is deeper and more encompassing. Hence a spiritual teacher, who has opened the higher chakras, can guide those of us who have not yet done so.

Each chakra is closely connected to a gland of the

endocrine system which monitors all the various functions of our being, including growth and health. Sluggish functioning of these glands will have a considerable influence in relation to our outlook on life, in respect to our moods, behaviour and ability to cope. We can become depressed, angry, fearful, or pessimistic; or happy, peaceful, confident and optimistic, depending on their condition. The glands are connected to the brain and from there to the emotional, mental and spiritual aspects of our being. In this way, the chakras are like conductors linking the various parts of our physical body where they are located, to the emotional or mental states associated with them. This is an example of a direct mind – body relationship.

COLOUR

Each chakra is also related to what are known as the seven colour rays, and specific illnesses relate to these rays. The colours of the rays and their associated chakras are:

Red: Mooladhara
Orange: Swadhisthana
Yellow: Manipura
Green: Anahata
Light Blue: Vishuddhi
Indigo Blue: Ajna
Violet: Sahasrara

The use of colour was well-known and incorporated by the ancient civilisations of China, Egypt, Greece and India. Usually the client would sit or lie quietly, bathed in the appropriate colour, or in a special room embedded with coloured precious stones that soothed and restored health. Alternatively, a practitioner, when placing his hands over an affected area, would visualise the appropriate colour as entering the body through his hands.

MERIDIANS

Out of ancient China has come a detailed description of the

meridians, energy pathways that criss-cross throughout the body, directly influencing our state of health. When there is a blockage anywhere on one of these pathways, energy cannot flow freely to the associated part of the body and illness can occur. Acupuncture uses needles (as fine as a strand of hair); acupressure uses physical pressure (an index finger or thumb in a fast circular movement) to stimulate points on these meridians. The resulting impulse goes to the brain and then back to the associated organ, freeing the blockage and restoring the energy flow.

The Chinese developed extensive diagrams of the meridians, as well as clear understandings of the nature of illness. Dis-eases were categorised according to the elements: earth, air, fire, water, and metal. Both acupuncture and acupressure can be extremely effective, and an understanding of the meridians helps to broaden our knowledge of the energy manifestations in the physical body.

Alongside these practices stands reflexology, also of Chinese origin. This is based on the meridians ending in the feet and hands, and forming "reflex" points that correspond to every part of the body. The left foot (or hand) reflects the left side, the right foot the right side, the spinal reflex running down the inside of each foot. The toes correspond to the head, the instep area to the digestive system and so on. Through deep pressure massage, energy can be released through the reflex points back into the associated part of the body. Where there is sickness, this helps to restore balance.

Out of reflexology has grown the Metamorphic Technique which also has its roots in ancient China. It has recognised that the spinal reflexes (in the feet, hands, on the head, and in the spine itself) not only correspond to the physical body but also correspond to our gestation period, from conception to birth. By a very light manipulation of these areas, energy that was blocked during this time period, and that is resulting in the reality we are now dealing with, can be loosened. It is not concerned with symptoms, and it allows the client to integrate the movement of energy in whatever way is needed. As with channelled healing work, the practitioner purposely stays out of the way and is simply a catalyst for change. By being detached in this way, the client has no restrictions imposed on his development. The work is done by the life force – that which is ever reaching towards greater levels of fulfilment.

Life is a factor that pervades, yet is beyond, everything. It is, and acts on, a power in matter and this power we call the life force. Life is creation and from creation comes movement: that movement is change, and it is the life force that sustains this change within the many differing cycles of existence ... the Metamorphic Technique stresses that even beyond this life force, the principle with which practitioners work is, simply, life. [9]

NUTRITION

Food provides our body with the essential nutrients needed for growth. If it does not receive these nutrients, it can fall sick. Very simple. Yet everyday we consume vast amounts of harmful products that contain very little nutrition and that we have come to think of as food, now more often referred to as junk. A basic, sane diet is therefore of primary importance.

Nature has generously provided us with an enormous variety of foods which, in their unadulterated state, give us exactly what we need to sustain good health. Yet the further removed we have become from nature, the more we have decided that these foods are only good to eat when processed to such an extent that they not only hardly resemble their original form, but they also no longer contain their original nutrition. Man is indeed a curious creature since somehow he has seen this separation from nature as progress! As a result, most of us are lacking in essential nutrients and are filling ourselves with harmful substitutes. Alternatively, we may continue to eat our junk food, simultaneously taking handfuls of vitamin and mineral supplements, in the blind hope of creating a balance. Obviously if we simplified our diet and began eating more as nature intended, none of the above would happen and our state of health would be remarkably improved.

Nature not only provided us with basic food in the way of grains, pulses, vegetables etc., but also gave us a vast array of natural medicines – herbs. The use of herbs for aiding in the recovery from virtually all known illnesses goes back many thousands of years. There is nothing new here, other than modern man's suspicion with regard to anything not man-made. Herbs can take longer to be effective than their chemical counterparts used in orthodox medicine, and this has frustrated people who want instant results. But there are fewer harmful side-effects with herbs, so they are generally a far safer form of medicine. Herbs and flowers (as in the Bach Flower Remedies) are used to treat the whole person, not just the symptoms that may have developed.

Naturopathy expands on both diet and the use of herbs by encouraging man to re-connect with his instinctive, original understanding of life. It includes massage, exercise, breathing, homoeopathy, nutrition, herbs, and a "use and application of all natural agencies and forces that may help to encourage not only better health but a return towards that state from one of ill-health."[10]

THERAPY

As seen earlier in this book, it soon becomes obvious that many of our difficulties may stem not just from recent stress, but also from stress that has accumulated over many years. This can be in the form of particular thought patterns or conditionings, ingrained since childhood, that have created a structure through which we live, thereby denying spontaneity or real development. A hurtful shock in the formative years may have induced us to build an emotional "armour" around ourselves so we are protected from further hurt, but which also stops us fully experiencing or expressing our feelings. Within all of us are deep, often denied, repressions of fear or insecurity that manifest in the various relationships and situations we create in our life and that cause dis-ease. There is a strong tendency to deny our darker side, to "push under the carpet" that which we do not like to see in ourselves, and to focus only on the nice, good, or socially acceptable qualities.

As we begin the process of self-discovery, we can then find ourselves actually discovering a Pandora's box, carefully hidden and full of shadowy figures. We could well be forgiven if we then begin to wonder if we were wise to start this journey after all! For to develop unconditional love may mean first having to recognise that deep down inside we do not really trust love; to develop humility and grace may mean first dealing with our hidden desires and unfulfilled longings. Denying that these feelings exist will create only a superficial sincerity and will add to the dis-ease already established.

Meditation and spiritual guidance is invariably the sanest way of dealing with this, but often help in the form of counselling or therapy can also aid us in coming to terms with, accepting, and loving what we find. We all need help along the path at various times, especially from those who have gone before us.

In my view therapy involves a voyage of self-discovery. It is not a short and simple journey, nor is it free from pain and hardship. There are dangers and risks, but then, life itself is not free from hazards, for it too, is a journey into the unknown of the future. Therapy takes us backward into a forgotten past, but this was not a safe and secure time, else we would not have emerged from it scarred by battle

101

wounds and armoured in self-defense. It is not a journey I would recommend to make alone, although I am sure some brave people have made the trip unaided. A therapist acts as a guide or navigator. He has been trained to recognise the dangers and he knows how to cope with them; he is also a friend who will offer support and courage when the going is rough. [11]

As there is an abundance of therapy techniques to choose from, we recommend a personal investigation to find that which is best suited. The most important factor to maintain is our goal – that of energy freely flowing throughout our physical, mental, emotional, and spiritual being, so that we become a unified whole. The means for reaching this goal will vary for each of us.

Healing through touch can enable an opening of our Pandora's box to take place, as we begin to let go of the inner stress and the patterns that formed it. At times, the specific help of counselling or therapy may therefore be needed, so we can deal with this more constructively. Alternatively we may find that our meditation practice and the guiding hand of a true master, is all we need to enable us to resolve our inner conflicts and emerge into a brighter world.

·8·
BENEFICIAL PRACTICES

This Chapter outlines relaxation, meditation, and visualisation techniques which can be practised to enable a deeper contact and relationship with inner peace i.e. with our own divinity. This is esential for true channelling and healing work. We cannot expect to go from our normal chaotic and confusing world to that of a healing practitioner without first quieting our mind. Surrendering to the divine is far from easy, as it first means having to look at that which is not divine, so these practices are the tools we can use to explore inwardly. As we practise, a state of stillness begins to pervade our being. Channelled energy is a natural expression of a still and quiet mind.

RELAXATION

When first learning how to relax, you may find it quite hard to be still for a period of twenty or thirty minutes, but if you persevere it soon becomes easier. To practice relaxation, first choose a time and place where you can be undisturbed. Make sure it is going to be warm enough, for as you relax and your body becomes quieter, so you may become slightly chilly. Cover yourself with a blanket to avoid this. Wear loose comfortable clothing with no tight belts, elastic, or jewellery.

Either lie on a mat or sit upright in a high-backed chair. Lying down is better but avoid lying on a bed as the tendency to sleep will be very strong. If a chair is preferred, it is best to

103

avoid a soft one for the same reason (sleepiness) and also because it will cause the spine to collapse. It is important that your spine be straight, which is its natural position (either vertical or horizontal). When truly straight, the chest and lungs are open and the muscles in your back do not have to work so can also relax.

Having become completely comfortable in your position, start by taking a few deep breaths. Most of us breathe unconsciously and only use the upper portion of our chest. Try instead not only to breathe with awareness of the flow of the air in and out, but also to breathe into the lower abdomen. This does not mean forced or prolonged breathing, but a deeper, fuller breath. Feel the rise and fall of your abdomen as you breathe in and out.

Now bring your attention to your right foot. Do not move, simply take your mind down into your right foot. Feel the toes. From the right foot, follow with attention up from the heel to the ankle, up the shin and calf, the right knee to the top of the right thigh. Take your time. Let your mind move slowly.

Now take your mind to the left foot and follow up through your left ankle, shin and calf, the left knee, to the top of the left thigh. Mentally enter into and discover each part of the body. Take time to do this. Feel each part of your body fully.

Now slowly become aware of your buttocks, the right buttock and the left buttock. Then become aware of the spine, slowly following up your entire spine to the shoulders. Become aware of the right and left sides of your back.

Next become aware of your abdomen and the whole belly region. Bring your awareness up through the right and left sides of the chest to the shoulders, slowly moving your awareness through your body. Your mind is completely at rest as you move from one part of your body to another.

Now go down into the right hand thumb, and from the thumb through all your fingers, the palm and back of the hand, to the wrist, forearm, elbow and upper arm. Mentally enter into the right armpit, and then your shoulder.

Now enter into the left hand thumb, into all the left hand fingers, the palm, back of hand, the left wrist, forearm, elbow, upper arm, the left armpit, and finally become aware of your left shoulder.

Now take your mind up through the neck to the face. Become aware of the jaw, chin, mouth, nose, cheeks, right and left eye, right and left eyebrow, forehead, right temple and right ear, left temple and left ear. Take your awareness around the back of your head and up to the crown.

Become aware of your whole body. Whole body awareness.

Feel yourself becoming heavy, sinking into the floor.

Now start at the right foot again, but this time tense the whole of your right foot and leg. Tense it so hard that it is lifted off the floor. Hold it, then let it go, move it around a little from side to side and forget about it.

Now become aware of your left leg. Then tense your left foot and leg so hard that it lifts off the floor. Hold it, then let it go, roll it around from side to side and forget about it.

Now tense the buttocks in the same way, hold the tension, then relax and let it go. Forget about them.

Then fill your stomach area with air, filling it up like a great balloon. Hold this tense balloon, then relax, letting the air rush out of your mouth. Then do the same with your chest, filling it with air, holding, then breathing out and letting go.

Now become aware of your right arm. Then tense the right hand and arm so tight that it lifts off the floor. Hold it, then let it go, roll it around a few times and forget about it.

Then take your awareness into your left arm, tensing the whole hand and arm as it lifts off the floor. Hold it, then relax, let it go and forget about it.

Then tense the shoulders, lifting them off the floor with tension. Lift them up to your neck, hold it, then relax and let go.

Move your head from side to side to release any tension. Then scrunch up your face into the ugliest face imaginable, tensing every muscle that there is, and then letting go.

Take a few deep breaths. Feel yourself sinking into the floor, becoming heavy. Letting go. Your whole body is relaxed and at ease.

Now bring your attention to your breath. Do not try to breathe in any unusual way, simply watch the flow of the natural breath. Watch it come in and go out. With every in-breath imagine you are breathing in calmness and peace; with every out-breath, imagine you are expelling tension and stress.

Then begin counting. As you breathe out begin to count at the end of each breath, mentally to yourself. Breathe in, breathe out, count to ten. Breathe in, breathe out, count to nine. Breathe in, breathe out, count to eight. Do this until you have reached nought. Then start at ten again and count back to nought. If you lose your counting, just start again at ten, and try to complete two rounds (10-0, 10-0) without losing your concentration.

After two rounds of counting, drop the counting and simply watch your breath. Thoughts will come and go, but pay no attention to them, keep your attention on your breath. Just witness that you are thinking. Witness the thoughts without holding on to them. Very shortly, you will find your mind becoming quiet and the thoughts less frequent. Your mind is now relaxing. Become one with your breath. Breathe into your abdomen, feeling the rise and fall of your stomach. You can stay like this as long as you want but be careful not to fall asleep. Sleeping is relaxation but without consciousness. Your aim is to relax consciously so you may enter into a state of quiet awareness.

When ready, become aware of your body and gently move your toes, feet, fingers, hands, legs, and arms. Sit up, then get up slowly. Stand still for a few minutes and listen. Open your eyes and look around. Are the noises and colours not somewhat brighter, sharper?

Now continue with your day, but witness your feelings and actions, and see if they are not just a little more gentle, selfless, and caring?

MEDITATION

Before starting any meditation practice, choose a time and place that allows for quiet, non-interference and optimum energy. The early morning is often preferred as the mind is fresh and unburdened. The evening is also good but can be a sleepy time. If you can, it is helpful to find a space in your home that can always be used, for after a while it will become a special place, one where you will be able to tune into your own energy, and you will not want it disturbed by other activities. If it is too dark, use a candle or soft light.

For any form of concentration or meditation, it is important that you sit with a straight back. Rather than lying down, which enhances the deeper relaxation state, here you are concerned with concentrating the mind, and an upright, alert position is required. This can be achieved by sitting either cross-legged on a cushion on the floor, or in a straight-backed hard chair. If in a chair, put your feet flat on the floor beneath you, your legs relaxed but not stretched out or crossed over. If sitting on the floor, you can adjust your cushions so that the spine is supported from below. Leaning against a wall does not achieve this. If your spine is not straight, it will soon bend over and begin to ache. Many Westerners find sitting cross-legged quite difficult, but practice makes perfect! In either position, the spine is erect. The hands are either folded in your lap or resting on your thighs. The head should feel like an extension of the spine, neither tilted up nor down. The mouth should be closed, and your eyes either left slightly open, looking down directly in front, or closed. If they are open, guard against being distracted; if they are closed, be careful not to fall asleep.

Most importantly you are comfortable but alert, erect but relaxed. After a while you will find yourself naturally concentrating as soon as you assume this posture.

It is better to practise for just ten minutes a day, if during that time you are concentrated, than to sit for an hour day-dreaming. Use your time well. Ten minutes a day, or even five to start with, will soon lengthen without you even realising it. By allowing the mind to concentrate, it will naturally move into a state of contemplation, and then meditation itself.

COUNTING BREATHS

This meditation is in three stages, so you may wish to time it, allowing approximately five to ten minutes for each stage, depending on how long you wish to practise.

Sit in your chosen position and preferably do not move during the practice. Breathe deeply a few times, relaxing as you do so. Throughout this whole practice breathe normally. The idea is simply to become aware of your breath, and to use it as a means for concentration, without purposefully changing it in any way.

In the first stage, count at the end of each breath. Breathe in, breathe out, count one. Breathe in, breathe out, count two. Breathe in, breathe out, count three. In this way, count up to ten. Then back to one again. Just count mentally to yourself. Continue counting like this at the end of each breath for the whole of the first stage.

If you lose your counting, or find you are counting beyond ten, then simply return to one and start again.

In the second stage, count at the beginning of each breath. Count in exactly the same way. Count one, breathe in, breathe out. Count two, breathe in, breathe out. Count three, breathe in, breathe out. Continue to ten, then back to one again. Although this may seem just like the first stage, your awareness has shifted and your concentration is deepening. From being aware of your breath after it has happened, you are now being aware of your breath before it has happened. If you lose your counting, just return to one again.

In the third stage, drop the counting and simply watch your breath. Watch it come in and go out. Allow it to flow. Concentrate on the breath, and become one with that flow.

Thoughts will come, but simply witness them and let them go, like clouds across the sky. Do not judge and do not become impatient for stillness takes time to develop. There is no point in having high expectations of yourself or you will feel disappointed. If this is practised every day, the benefits will be felt very quickly.

To finish, gently move your body, open your eyes if they are closed, take a few deep breaths and sit quietly aware for a few moments before getting up.

SOHAM

For this technique start in the same way; become comfortable in your seated position, and take a few deep breaths to relax. Then begin to become aware of your breathing, watching the flow.

Focus on the breath as it enters the nostrils, fills your abdomen and leaves again.

Now, as you breathe in say, mentally to yourself: SO. As you breathe out say: HAM (pronounced hum). This is the sound of your breath. Allow the words to flow with your breath – in: SO; out: HAM. *SOHAM*. There should be no separation between them. It is very important that you maintain awareness at all times as this is not a mechanical recitation.

It is also helpful if, during this practice, you fix your attention on either the third-eye centre (between the eyebrows) or on the heart centre (the heart). From here simply watch your breath flowing in and out. Thus you have a combination of endurance, awareness, focusing, breathing, relaxation, and concentration. You are physically still and mentally quiet but alert. Maintain *soham* with each breath.

After a while stop repeating *soham* and simply focus on the breath. Witness any thoughts that come, but do not hold on to them. Witness the quiet. Watch the breath and focus on stillness.

Then begin doing the *soham* again, mentally reciting the words as you breathe in and out. The words fill your being and you become one with them.

At the end of the practice sit quietly for a few moments, simply being present here and now before moving. You can do this practice for any amount of time that you wish to.

WALKING MEDITATION

If you are practising meditation quite often, your legs may get very tired and cause discomfort, at least until you are used to the seated position. In the East, where they squat or sit cross-legged all the time, they have no such problems. We have spent our lives in armchairs and it can take a while to retrain our body. Therefore the following practice is very helpful. It is meditation in action. At all times maintain your concentration on your breath, but at the same time begin to walk, very slowly, watching the movement.

Firstly stand upright and still. Bring your hands together in front, arms bent at the elbow, so the hands are held in front of the solar plexus, at a level that causes no strain to your arm muscles. The right hand should be held gently over the left hand, close to the body. Eyes should be kept open but focused only on the floor directly in front of you.

Now begin to walk, very slowly. Feel each step, the movement that takes place throughout the whole body as you lift, move and re-place each foot. Your concentration remains on your breath, with the addition of the movement.

The walking and the breathing flow together. Your eyes focus only on the floor.

You can walk like this, either going round a relatively empty room or outside in a garden, for fifteen to twenty minutes if you want to. When you sit down to meditate again, you will find that your energies are sharper, more awake and alert.

VISUALISATION

Visualisation can be of many things, colours, or forms. Two practices have been included here and both are fairly detailed, but you can simplify this easily if you want to.

Always do visualisation in a state of alert mindfulness, having first taken the right posture (as already described) and then having relaxed and quietened the mind. In creating your own visualisation, it is important to remain focused and concentrated – changing the image too quickly will give no time for integration or full experience. It is better to choose just one image to focus on in any one session. A religious symbol, a colour, a beautiful landscape, or white light, are some examples.

Stay with the image as long as possible, allowing your mind to become fully concentrated. Let the thoughts come and go. Simply witness and return to the practice. When you are ready, gently dissolve the image and stay sitting quietly for a few moments in a state of stillness before moving.

FIVE ELEMENTS

This practice combines colour, visualisation, and energy states together. It is important to practise it sitting upright and not lying down. Allow about five minutes for each stage so that the whole practice will last about thirty-five to forty minutes.

111

First find a comfortable but erect and alert posture, as already outlined. Take a few deep breaths and relax.

Now focus your mind on visualising a clear blue sky. The sky fills your entire mind. It is completely clear, almost transparent, a beautiful blue.

Within the clear blue sky now visualise a yellow cube. Not just a square, but a complete cube. It is yellow and symbolises earth. Earth energy is solid, heavy, unmoving, and you feel this type of energy within yourself. Become the earth.

On top of the yellow cube now visualise a white sphere, completely round. This symbolises water. Water moves freely, but only horizontally, so feel this energy movement within yourself, from earth now to water, moving horizontally.

Next visualise a red pyramid on top of the white sphere. This symbolises fire. The energy of fire moves upward, so feel that change in yourself as the energy moves from water to fire, from horizontal to vertical.

Then visualise a shallow green bowl (half moon) on top of the red pyramid. This symbolises air. Air can pervade in all directions. Your energy flows with the air energy.

In the green bowl now visualise a shining, shimmering, multi-coloured jewel. This jewel symbolises consciousness, that moves not only in all directions, but can pervade everywhere, even passing through matter. Feel your energy change as you move into a state of pure consciousness.

After approximately five minutes begin to dissolve the jewel back into the clear blue sky.

Then dissolve the green saucer into the sky.

Then dissolve the red pyramid.

Next slowly dissolve the white sphere, followed by the yellow cube, dissolving into the clear blue sky.

Now stay with your empty, clear blue sky for a few minutes longer. Any thoughts that come are simply like clouds that pass through without stopping.

Finally dissolve the clear blue sky and the practice is over.

SELF-HEALING

This is a beautiful visualisation that enables a deeper understanding of illness and healing. As we explore our healing ability we can find many different sensations or visions coming to us. This practice helps us to understand them. It is based on the idea that physical disorders are actually trying to tell us something about ourselves. They are an expression of conflict on another, non-physical level.

Do this practice lying down, covered with a blanket to keep warm. Start by spending a few minutes relaxing and breathing deeply. Relax completely. Relax every part of your body and mind, becoming quiet and concentrated.

Now imagine you are getting smaller and smaller, until you are small enough to walk around inside your body.

Begin to explore your body from the inside. Be systematic – start at the feet and work very slowly up through every part of the body. If you come to an area of pain, discomfort, tension or dis-ease, then stop and explore that area.

Then ask what colour is the discomfort? Is it dark or light, does it have a colour? What texture is it? Does it feel soft or hard, sponge-like or spiky? How big is it? Does it change from one colour or texture to another?

As you ask the questions, let the answers come of their own accord. If there is no answer, that's fine, just ask another question. Stay lying quietly, with your eyes closed, and continue to explore.

When you begin to get answers, ask more questions.

You can ask what is it the pain is trying to tell you?

What is it that it would like you to do, to help it feel better?

What needs to be done in order for it to be free to go?

What is its purpose?

If you can, begin a dialogue with the pain, always allowing it to speak for itself. It may take a while for it to respond. If that is the case then, as you leave, you can arrange to come back and talk some more another time. Set up a time and day when you will return, and make sure you keep your word. At the appointed hour, repeat this procedure and begin again to explore and ask questions inside yourself.

When you feel you have your answers, say thank you. Come back out of your body and grow larger again until you fit back into yourself. If you can, it is helpful to write down all the answers you have received, and then take your time to integrate them. They will be telling you about yourself. Do not judge. Remember to love yourself at all times.

IN CONCLUSION

Learning is an interesting process as often we can only do it by un-learning what we have already learned. We spend our lives collecting a vast assortment of knowledge and information, only to find that it can then get in the way and we have to let it all go, in order to find ourselves buried beneath. In discovering our latent healing ability, so we have to find this hidden self and become more deeply in contact with it. In Zen Buddhism there is the phrase 'beginner's mind' and it is this attitude of the beginner, of simplicity, openness, receptivity and unknowingness, that enables us to proceed. Through acceptance, love, and a letting go of personal gratification, we can become truly compassionate and wise.

REFERENCES

1. H. Motoyama (ed.), P.K. "Influence on the Meridians and Psi-Energy", *Research for Religion and Psychology*, 4-11-7 Inokashisa, Mitaka-Shi, Tokyo 181, Japan. Vol. 5, No. 2, July 1979.

2. Prof. J.B. Hasted M.A., D.Phil., "Paranormal Electrical Effects", Dept. of Physics, Birkbeck College, University of London, Malet Street, London WCIE 7HX, UK.

3. Refer to A. Montague, *Touching. The Human Significance of the Skin*, Harper & Row.

4. Ibid.

5. Reshad, Field, *Here to Heal*, Element Books, 1985.

6. Ibid.

7. Ibid.

8. Gaston Saint Pierre and Debbie Boater, *The Metamorphic Technique*, Element Books, 1982.

9. Ibid.

10. *British Naturopathic Association Journal*.

11. A. Lowen, *Bioenergetics*, Coventure.